My wife and I have been the d  ledge
and practice of the phenomeno ly en-
dorse this book. It's fully practi or ev-
ery parent, grandparent, and godparent looking child's
life development. Thank you, Bill and Bev. You have blessed us immensely
with this one!

**EVAN & STACIE NICOLE SIMMONS,** President & Vice President, One in
Christ Jesus International Ministries

As an administrator of a school for more than thirty years, I would place
this book on my must-read to every parent and grandparent in my school.
It's that important and insightful! This delightful book is like being on a
treasure hunt and you find out that the treasure is YOU!

**MARY HELEN NOLAND,** Director of Admissions at Trinity Christian Academy

As a raving fan and former client of The Giftedness Center, *So How Do
I Parent This Child?* answered my prayers as I've wanted to replicate my
transformation to help my young daughter discover her unique giftedness
pattern. This book gives me a blueprint to do just that!

**BAILEY HEARD**

I began reading this book with the idea that it would help me be a better
*abuelita* (grandmother) for baby Tatum. I know it will do that and much
more because of my own search for purpose in my "empty nest" stage of
life. This is a great gift for parents, grandparents, and anyone working with
children!

**ANNA REYES AGNEW,** Giftedness Center client, friend, and new *abuelita*

Bev and Bill show us how to foster proven competence in our children
instead of defaulting to the mediocre world of participation trophies
found in today's society. I thought kids arrived without owner's manuals.
Turns out it was right there in plain sight, but in a different language that
I couldn't read—until now!

**NEWT FARRAR**

This is a precious resource, especially for us as parents of a son with complex and long-term medical conditions. It helps us to look beyond his
needs and discover and affirm his unique giftedness, intended to bless
this world.

**ANDREW AND JEANNETTE FENG**

Therapists, students, educators, and certainly parents will find themselves benefiting from having their perspectives broadened by the unique approach of this book. No longer will the question be, "What's wrong with this/my child?" but rather, each person who hopes to play a significant role in a young person's life will be challenged to ask, "What is *right* about this/my child?" As a therapist and counselor educator specializing in child development, this book caused me to pause and reflect on the bents of each of my own children. This resource will be a valuable tool as I train future counselors. It brings freedom in normalizing differences and celebrates the beautiful gifts in each child.

**ANDI THACKER,** Assistant Professor of Biblical Counseling, Dallas Theological Seminary

Bill and Bev's work in human giftedness has been instrumental in our passion of mentoring young adults. Now these universal truths are brought to life for parents in this groundbreaking work of how to raise children within the framework of abilities and joy.

**BILL BOGART AND KIT CASE,** Case & Bogart, LLC

What an insightful and thought-provoking book! I wish I had been able to read it when my kids were young. I've never seen this in any of the parenting books I read.

**JOHN ENGLISH,** Founder, Bethesda Medical Clinic

This is a great book! The practical application of understanding and honoring giftedness in our children makes this a must-read for every parent. And dads especially need this in their toolbox. Love your child! Read this book!

**ALEX VASQUEZ**

As a dedicated mom and classroom teacher of my own children, I thought I really "knew" them until I encountered the information in this book. The stories and insights in it are unlike anything you'll encounter in other parenting books. Discovering our children's giftedness proved to be pivotal in choosing their life's fulfilling work. Today, they know their purpose and where their energy and giftedness should be applied for making a meaningful and fulfilling impact.

**LYNDA MARTIN**

I'm going to need an endless supply of *So How Do I Parent This Child?* to give out to friends. I once took Bill to coffee to ask him how I could start supporting my elementary-age son, Caleb, and what you'll find in this book is what Bill shared with me—practical principles that will be a blessing to any family.

**KAT ARMSTRONG,** Cofounder, The Polished Network and author of *No More Holding Back* and *The In-Between Place*

Sometimes we say we are standing on the shoulders of those who have gone before. This is definitely a must-read that stands on the heart of those who have gone before! Bill and Bev have blown through decades of old, cliché parenting advice and brought us a fresh perspective on raising our kids based on biblical wisdom and a child's particular giftedness. It doesn't surprise me a bit that this great resource is born from the incredible legacy of Howard ("Prof") and Jeanne Hendricks.

**GREG HATTEBERG,** Executive Director of Alumni Services, Dallas Theological Seminary

Two generations of our family have benefited from the wisdom of Bill Hendricks and Bev Godby in helping all of us discover our unique giftedness. As a family, we hope our experience of learning to understand the way God designed each of us with core strengths and natural motivations will become yours, as well, through this book. "Giftedness is not just what you can do, but what you are born to do, enjoy doing, and do well."

**FRED SMITH JR.,** Founder, The Gathering

Bill and Bev have "gifted" to us a powerful tool that helps our children understand how their lives matter. I owe a debt of gratitude to Bill for helping me discover at fifty my unique giftedness, and now I have a method to pass that gift on to my children and grandchildren. This book and *The Person Called You* are two of the most important books you could ever read!

**DAVID W. BALL, MD,** Internal Medicine

Another book on parenting? Yes, but whereas most books on child development leave parents with a cloud of guilt and a few pointers on crowd control and how to send the little urchins down the assembly line, the magic of this book is that it teaches parents to study their child and point them in the direction of the person God intended them to be—giving them a lifelong vision for their unique role in this world.

**BEN ALBRITTON,** Psychologist

No matter the situation, that little one you hold happens to be a declarative statement of "Yes, this is meant to be." All of it—this child, exactly as they are made, and you the parent, with everything you have and are, as well as everything you don't have and aren't—is joined together in a narrative of purpose that has been planned from eternity and is beginning to live itself out right here, right now before your very eyes. What a privilege to be chosen to participate in the revelation of such a promise!

**DONNA WEBER**

The scales have fallen from my eyes! I now am beginning to see AND understand the ways in which my kids are GIFTED with wonderful abilities, talents, and capabilities that MOTIVATE them. These customized PATTERNS are the road map to their thriving and contentment. Bev and Bill, thank you for this incredible, easy-to-understand and apply book. I needed this twenty years ago!

**TIM WEBER**

Several members of our family have worked with Bill and Bev to discover their giftedness, and through that their purpose and calling. Now they are giving parents a way to begin that discovery process at home, and from their children's earliest years. The insights gained from giftedness have made such a difference for our family. I know it can do the same for yours.

**ROBERT AND MAGGIE MURCHISON**

I have long admired the authors of this book and I am so pleased that siblings, Bill Hendricks and Bev Godby, have written this most insightful book. Their dad, the late Professor Howard Hendricks, would be so proud of them. In *So How Do I Parent This Child?*, they skillfully portray the uniqueness in each child's "giftedness." This book's call to understand and embrace that "giftedness" is an invitation for parents to be sharpened in how they raise their children, ultimately so that each child may be all that God desires for them to be. The wisdom that they impart will be helpful for all Christian parents who want to train up their children in the way that they should go.

**GARY COOK,** Chancellor and former president, Dallas Baptist University, Dallas, TX

*How Do I Parent This Child?* achieves a rare feat: it is both a practical guide for parenting and a map for understanding my own giftedness and motivation.

**STEVE RAMSEUR,** Corporate Executive

Bill and Bev Hendricks have made their life's work the study of giftedness—helping thousands discover how they were uniquely created to live and flourish in the world. In How do I Parent This Child? Bill and Bev lay out the tools parents need to uncover the wonder of their child's giftedness. I'd give this book to any parent eager to shepherd their child toward a life rich with purpose and meaning.

**PEGGY WEHMEYER,** Reporter for ABC News

# so how do i parent *this* child?

## Discovering the Wisdom & Wonder of Who Your Child Was Meant to Be

**BILL HENDRICKS** AND
**BEV HENDRICKS GODBY**

NORTHFIELD PUBLISHING
CHICAGO

Scripture quotations taken from the (NASB®) New American Standard Bible®, Copyright © 1960, 1971, 1977, 1995, 2020 by The Lockman Foundation. Used by permission. All rights reserved. www.lockman.org.

Scripture quotations marked (NIV) are taken from the Holy Bible, New International Version®, NIV®. Copyright © 1973, 1978, 1984, 2011 by Biblica, Inc.™ Used by permission of Zondervan. All rights reserved worldwide. www.zondervan.com The "NIV" and "New International Version" are trademarks registered in the United States Patent and Trademark Office by Biblica, Inc.™

Scriptures marked NET are from the NET Bible® http://netbible.com copyright ©1996, 2019 used with permission from Biblical Studies Press, L.L.C. All rights reserved.

Edited by Elizabeth Cody Newenhuyse
Interior design: Puckett Smartt
Cover design: Erik M. Peterson
Cover photo of group of children copyright © 2021 by Ariel Skelley/Getty Images (200533169-001). All rights reserved.
Bill Hendricks photo: Dave Edmonson
Bev Hendricks Godby photo: Nancy Lovell

Library of Congress Cataloging-in-Publication Data

Names: Hendricks, William, 1954- author. | Godby, Bev Hendricks, author.
Title: So how do I parent this child? : discovering the wisdom & wonder of
   who your child was meant to be / Bill Hendricks and Bev Hendricks Godby.
Description: Chicago : Northfield Publishing, [2021] | Includes
   bibliographical references. | Summary: "Parenting books often suggest
   that parents determine how their children turn out. The truth is, your
   child has unique traits-their giftedness-that only they possess. Your
   job as a parent isn't to engineer a product, but to identify your
   child's gifts and steward them toward a mature, fruitful life"--
   Provided by publisher.
Identifiers: LCCN 2021022033 | ISBN 9780802422132 (paperback) | ISBN
   9780802499349 (ebook)
Subjects: LCSH: Parenting. | Parent and child. | Personality in children. |
   Ability in children | BISAC: FAMILY & RELATIONSHIPS / Parenting /
   General | FAMILY & RELATIONSHIPS / Military Families
Classification: LCC HQ755.8 .H4647 2021 | DDC 649/.1--dc23
LC record available at https://lccn.loc.gov/2021022033

We hope you enjoy this book from Northfield Publishing. Our goal is to provide high-quality, thought-provoking books and products that connect truth to your real needs and challenges. For more information on other books and products that will help you with all your important relationships, go to northfieldpublishing.com or write to:

Northfield Publishing
820 N. LaSalle Boulevard
Chicago, IL 60610

1 3 5 7 9 10 8 6 4 2

*Printed in the United States of America*

# dedication

### From Bill:

*This book is dedicated to
every parent who keeps showing up for your child.
May this book encourage you that that the effort is worth it
because your child has infinite worth.*

### From Bev:

*And to Liam, Hayden, Tess, Cameran, Shepherd, and Lake*

*"We will tell the next generation the praiseworthy deeds of the Lord,
his power, and the wonders he has done." Psalm 78:4 NIV*

# contents

## Part IV: The Teenage Years

## Part V: Getting Ready for Liftoff

# an invitation

t was the usual day in Mrs. Simpkins's class. Fifth graders slumped over wooden desks, overseen from the front of the room by a figure who glared at them as they toiled over their seatwork, ever attentive to spot the slightest infraction of her rules.

They were bored. She was bored. *Surely it must be time for lunch,* she thought, mildly cheered by the prospect. She glanced up to check the clock when a spit wad, guided by the kind of telemetry that can only be attained by carefully honed skill, smacked her desk with a pinpoint landing right in the middle of her open book.

## An Entertaining Distraction

"Come up here!" No name was needed. She knew. So did the entire class. All eyes zeroed in on row three, way in the back of the room. There sat a small boy, exiled by Mrs. Simpkins with the failed notion that perhaps if hidden out of sight from the others, his influence would do less harm.

The boy rose and began sauntering his way forward, self-assured and nodding slyly to all his co-conspirators. But just then, the lunch bell rang, at last signaling sweet freedom for everyone.

Everyone, that is, except the unfortunate boy. Refusing to own up to the crime or be sufficiently shamed for it, he now faced the corner with indifference. One thing he knew for sure: he hated Mrs. Simpkins as much as she hated him. Indeed, there was nothing he loved so much as to figure out new ways to make her world spin out of control. He had become a master at it. Whatever he could find—erasers, paper clips, pencils—in his hands they became stealth missiles launched to destroy her command of the classroom and bring his comrades a measure of distraction.

## The Professor Extraordinaire

My father, a consummate storyteller, recounted this story from his distant childhood with such energy and recall of detail that the incident might easily have happened the day before.

I (Bev) had gone to see him one afternoon in the early fall to see if he could give me some inspiration for a talk I had been asked to make to a middle school faculty on the topic, "How to Keep a New School Year from Being Just Another Year." Since he was about to begin his own fifty-ninth year of teaching, I figured, who better to ask?

I knew there was no place Dad would rather be than in front of a class of students—unless it was in his red overstuffed chair at home, absorbed in preparing for that class. Because of that, I was confident he would give me something valuable. But I didn't expect this story of fifth-grade fame—or notoriety.

"I spent most of that year in every corner of the room," he told me, "and I'm pretty sure that lady saw education in my future. But I think it was more along the lines of a reform school than a theological seminary!"

## "I've Heard All About You!"

He told me that, mercifully, his year in Mrs. Simpkins's prison class finally ended, and he did what he could to make the best of an all-too-brief summer break. But come the fall it was back in jail again. His assigned teacher for sixth grade was a Miss Noe. On the first day of classes he timed his entrance to her room for the last possible second, his goal being to slink unseen into a free desk at the very back of the room, parked next to a cadre of his buddies.

But to his surprise, a tiny woman darted into the classroom just behind him, swiftly closed the door, followed him down the aisle, allowed him to take his seat, then stood right in front of his desk. "Howard Hendricks," she said. The room fell silent. "I've heard all about you."

Never mind that my dad was sitting right across from me. I could see in his eyes that he was right back in that classroom, reliving that moment of suspense, just waiting for what Miss Noe was going to say next. "I was thinking to myself, *Oh boy! Here we go. Okay, lady, just bring it on.* Except then she looked right down at me—and smiled! Which, believe me, *that* was rare enough! But then she went on: 'I've heard all about you. But you know, I don't believe a word of it. What I believe is this: *you* are exactly the person we most need in our class this year. I am so looking forward to having you. Welcome to sixth grade!'"

My Dad shook his head with that memory. "I have to tell you, Bevsils, I was completely caught off guard! But I'm telling you, from that day on I was hooked!"

### "One of My Best Students . . . and a Leader"

After that, there was nothing Howard Hendricks wouldn't do for Miss Noe. He came to school early and stayed late, offering to help his teacher with any chores she might have. During the school day she often sent him on errands outside the classroom. He told me that was his very favorite thing to do because then all the other kids could see for themselves how much she counted on him.

Then one day came the *pièce de résistance*, Dad said. Miss Noe was standing in the hall before class, talking to—of all people—Mrs. Simpkins. As he walked by, he overheard Miss Noe saying to his former teacher, "Howard Hendricks? Oh no, he's one of my best students! And what a leader he is in my class!"

Dad laughed at the memory. "I was just perverse enough to turn around and flash Simpkins the biggest smirk I could manage. I just totally enjoyed the shock written all over her face!"

## What Is Right with This Child?

This story turned out to be so much more than a whimsical tale from my father's early escapades. As improbable as it may seem, these two different faces of the same boy turn out to be hallmark illustrations of my dad's giftedness. That's right, his *giftedness*—the unique way he was born to function. From his earliest years, my father would come to life and be at his best whenever he could get people to respond to him, whenever he could make an impact on them, and whenever he could become a part of a cherished group or team. That was a pattern in his life—a pattern he followed until the day he died.

Mrs. Simpkins and Miss Noe both observed the same young Howard. But they viewed him through radically different lenses. Mrs. Simpkins chose a lens of disappointment. She cast him as the disrupter, the problem child, the budding criminal to be banished to the back row. Predictably, Howard gained enormous satisfaction and energy from living down to those expectations. So much so that he became her worst nightmare—to his total delight. In no time at all, he wasn't playing a game, he was playing *her*. The angrier she got, the more he relished the response. Never mind that the response was negative. He had a whole audience of classmates who applauded his shenanigans— the more outrageous, the better!

Miss Noe, on the other hand, viewed young Howard very differently. Despite Howard's reputation—which I can only imagine was infamous among the teachers at that school—Miss Noe chose from the outset to give him the response he yearned for. I am guessing that this shrewd teacher, whether from intuition or experience, believed there was much more packed into that misbehaving child than just his antics. She wisely determined to key in on what was *right* with him.

I will always be curious to know how she had the foresight to do that, to make it her priority to engage the best of that little firebrand from day one. Whatever her secret, she was savvy enough to know exactly how to win him over. Not by changing him, but rather by changing her approach to him. By being willing to believe there was treasure in him that no one had yet bothered to find and celebrate (in truth, no one had). She let him know she was ready to value and respect him for exactly who he was.

### "I Live to Teach!"

Ever since that memorable afternoon with my dad, his words have stuck in my mind: "more along the lines of a reform school than a theological seminary." He could have gone either way. So what happened to make the difference for that little boy as he stood at such a pivotal crossroad? More than anything else at that vulnerable moment, he desperately needed a champion who could see what was right with him. Someone to be present to the wonder of who he was—mischief and all. Miss Noe providentially turned out to be the guardian angel who showed up for him. In doing so, she changed the course of his life—and through him, the lives of countless others, as well. Thanks to Miss Noe, Howard grew up to be a man who frequently declared, "I love to teach! I *live* to teach! Why, I'd teach whether or not they paid me to teach!" At which point he'd usually murmur as an aside, "Don't tell the seminary that!"

**He desperately needed a champion who could see what was right with him.**

But it was true! The man could not *not* teach. And to this day it's impossible to account for all the lines of impact that have flowed into this world through my father, thanks in part to the path he took as a result of Miss Noe's singular influence. Tens of thousands of students. Millions who listened to his messages and read his books. And of course our own family and its rising generations.

That's why this book is very personal to me and to my brother, Bill. It's a book about giftedness, which means it's about story. A person's giftedness is discovered through their story, their lived experience. We watched our father live out his giftedness every day. And the older we get, the more thankful we are that Miss Noe watched it, too, and at a critical moment set it on a different path, with a different outcome. Because our own stories have so much depended on his.

## The Wonder That Is Your Child

G. K. Chesterton once observed, "The world will never starve for want of wonders; but only for want of wonder."[1] I don't know exactly what brings you to this book, but I assume it's because a child you care about has brought you. More than anything else, this book is going to keep asking you: How acutely are you seeing the wonder of that child?

Wonder may at first seem beside the point. You may already be overwhelmed trying to raise a child, having crash-landed into an all-consuming world of information overload. You've consulted all the experts, and all it's done is create massive anxiety about the "right" way to parent. You're thinking, *Who's got time for wonder?*

It may be that you're raising a child who is not your own. You're part of that larger family or village that sometimes steps in to take up the responsibility for a child whose natural parents no longer can. Perhaps you're looking for fresh ideas and encouragement. But wonder? That's not something you've considered.

Then again, you may be someone who engages children as part of your profession or avocation, like Miss Noe. It may well be that you have a heart and passion for that work, but you get precious little validation, appreciation, or support for your service. That can prove challenging! So what you need is food for your soul, along with resources that will help you in that work you already do so well.

But no matter who you are or how you've come upon this book or what you are hoping to find in it, it may be that the little child who lives inside of you is the person who most needs its message. We all begin there, as a little child, helpless and at the mercy of the world that receives us. And no matter what else happens for a person in their life, that child is still waiting inside of each of us, longing to know the deepest truth of who they are is seen and celebrated. That's really what this book is about.

**It may be that the little child who lives inside of you is the person who most needs its message.**

Years ago I (Bev) had the privilege of hearing Madeleine L'Engle speak at a creative writing conference. As she concluded her final presentation, she surprised us by announcing that it was her seventy-sixth birthday. She then invited us to celebrate with her by saying these wise words: "You are all of the ages you have ever been. They reside very much alive inside of you. And it is a gift to go back and cherish the memory of who you were at a particular age. Because the older we get, the more easily we can forget those reflections of our younger, carefree selves. Children can lead us back to that understanding we once had that we may have rejected or forgotten. If I can retain a child's awareness and joy and be seventy-six years of age, then I will truly have learned what it means to be grown-up."

## Listening and Seeing

Bill and I have a consulting practice called The Giftedness Center. We help people discover their giftedness, which among other things means reclaiming the good truth about who they are and why they are here in this space and time. That insight allows them to choose life—that is, to make intentional decisions about their work and their relationships that lead to living on purpose and with purpose, all the days they are given.

Our work involves listening to certain kinds of stories from a person's life journey—ones that showcase some of the best moments of their life. From that simple storytelling exercise we can show them a unique pattern of core, instinctive functioning that proves consistently satisfying. It's their "sweet spot," the place that is truly home for them. It's where they operate at their best and where they experience a deeply affirming surge of energy and fulfillment.

In listening to the stories, we often find that a person's childhood stories are particularly revealing, perhaps because they take us back to a child who was just doing with contentment what they naturally loved to do and chose to do at that age, apart from anyone's judgment. Sometimes the activity they were doing in the story turns out to be a metaphor for how they approach all of life.

It's sobering, however, to discover that all too often, the person has never told those cherished stories to anyone. No one else has ever had the delight of seeing them in that early morning light of childhood. No one has ever watched the joy on their face as they recall the details that still mean the world to them. No one has ever witnessed the tears that sometimes come in remembering significant people who loved and shaped them in their youth. So to serve as their audience while they recount some of the signature moments of their life—that's among the highest and most humbling privileges of our work. For us, it underscores the deep need *each* of us has to be seen and known and valued for the unique person only we could ever be.

There is indeed no want of wonders! Wonders are waiting to be discovered in every person you'll ever encounter. There are wonders in the child you care about. And there are also wonders in you, infinitely alive in your own sacred stories.

So I invite you to come with us and spend some time in the presence of wonder, seeing the world come alive through the eyes of a child. And it just may be, that certain slant of light may forever change the way you look at everything else.

# PART I

# your purpose as a parent

# 1

# meant to be

The party had begun in Room 540. The guest of honor was front and center, his tiny head swathed in a headband with a gigantic bow that someone thought was cute. The rest of him was swaddled in a generic hospital blanket that his mother couldn't wait to replace. He was perfection, that's for sure—this bundle of wonder, so still and enchanting.

While the little rock star insisted on slumbering through his welcome, his fans were in full celebratory form. The entourage of family could not get enough of their newest member as they obsessed over staring at the baby, holding the baby, posing with the baby. Everyone's joy felt complete.

## A "Problem"

Then a kindly hospital worker came into the room, "Just to do a brief screening on the baby's hearing," she explained. The din quieted down as she went to work, bending over the crib several times in an attempt to "get a good reading." When at last she looked up, a roomful of stares made it plain she was expected to report on her findings. "He passed the test in one ear," she announced, "but not on the other side. That's not a problem. I'll come back tomorrow and check him again." And with that she turned and left.

The baby bliss didn't take long to fade. The word "problem" lingered in the air like some unwelcome guest who had suddenly shown up and was now sucking all the euphoric oxygen out of the festivities. Dismay and worry broke out, leading to endless discussion about what it could mean for baby to have failed the hearing test. That, in turn, led to more speculation as to which lineage had passed on a history of hearing loss. And finally, what would this new development mean for the child growing up?

> **Nothing is worse than being told that there is something wrong with your precious child.**

The new mother's mother tried to right the ship by contributing her knowledge as a former healthcare professional, reminding everyone—most especially her daughter—how unreliable these screening tests could often be, especially in the early days after birth. They could be erroneously affected by any number of variables. Take the simple fact that he had been born three weeks early. Blah, blah, blah.

But no amount of logical reasoning stood a ghost of a chance of prevailing against the emotional uncertainty of that moment. The mother of the child had received distressing news. And for any mother, nothing is worse than being told, in effect, that there is something wrong with your precious child. Not on the day of his birth, nor on any day before or after. Any mention of a problem cannot be unheard. That moment is felt as a gut punch of fear, followed by a lingering nausea about how little control a parent ultimately has over all the possible things that can happen to their child.

## Meant to Be

Yet right here, even in that fog of fear and uncertainty, is the best news we could possibly give you. No matter the situation, that little one you hold happens to be a declarative statement of, "Yes, this is meant to be." All of it—this child, exactly as they are made, and you the parent, with everything you have and are, as well as everything you don't have and aren't—is joined together in a narrative of purpose that has been planned from eternity and is beginning to live itself out right here, right now before your very eyes. What a privilege to be chosen to participate in the revelation of such a promise!

But that's not all. There are indelible fingerprints displayed in the unique workmanship crafted into every single person. They are evidence of an intentional design, made for just this space and time. William Wordsworth eloquently described that mystery with the poetic words, "But trailing clouds of glory do we come, from God, who is our home: Heaven lies about us in our infancy."[1]

Those "clouds of glory" show up in a person's *giftedness*—the unique way in which they were made to do life. A person's giftedness is like the explanatory notes that accompany a painting in a museum. Or like an owner's manual for how the person is designed to function.

## The Why, the Story, and the Joy

Parenting is a long journey of faithfulness in the same direction, but there are no guarantees as to where that journey will go. Nevertheless, the more you can understand about the giftedness of your child, the more you'll be able to come up with wise, intentional choices that make sense for *that* child. Every day, with every encounter, you create the kind of relationship you will have with your child for a lifetime. So here are some ways in which giftedness can provide you with a solid framework for that all-important work.

1. *Giftedness gives you a glimpse into the why for your child.* Every baby is here on purpose, for purpose, to be for this time and space as the very person they are born to be. You must never lose sight of

that truth. While there will always be a combination of factors affecting your child's path in life, their giftedness remains the central factor. That returns them home and that lets you know what is most *right* with your child.

Like the stars, your child emanates light. That light may flicker at times, but it always embodies the splendor of a radiance that is all their own. So when you devote time to observing your child's behavior and watching their path over time, you become more attentive to the great wonder of their presence in your life, and to the joy they display in shining their own brightness, exactly as it was meant to be.

2. *Giftedness reminds you of the power of story.* You as a parent have been invited into your child's story, not as the author, but as the trusted representative of the grace that holds your child. You do that by responsibly caring for their needs and shepherding their heart on the path of life, always with the goal of extending radical, unconditional hospitality.

Whether you or your spouse gave birth to your little one, or whether you brought them into your home through fostering, adoption, or some other committed relationship, be aware that your role in their life will always take you back to the immutable truth of their personhood. You don't make that personhood; it comes written into your child's being. That reality should inspire a deep humility, as well as a deep desire for discernment as you contemplate the part you are being asked to play in your child's story. Your presence in it is privileged, and with each and every interaction you have with your child, it is good to remind yourself that you are standing on the holy ground of unique giftedness. Everything you do there matters.

3. *Giftedness is an engraved invitation to joy.* You can read all the child-rearing manuals you will, listen to as many podcasts as

you wish, and absorb as much well-intended advice from other parents as you can handle, but none of that can ever replace the initial wonder and overwhelming gratitude you had at that first moment when you fell in love with this one-of-a-kind person you now know as your child. That child's giftedness will reveal the extraordinary treasure of who they are, restoring you to "gladness of heart" on the days when you weather the very real doubts and demands that come with being a parent. As you watch your child take in the beauty and loveliness of this world for the first time with delight, you discover they are calling *you* to taste and see the goodness of this life as never before, inspiring you to enter each new day with expectancy and hope.

The Why. The Story. The Joy. Think of these three pieces as the scaffolding that supports you in being the parent you most want to be and who your child needs you to be.

After that, most everything else about parenting is improvisational art. There's no definitive "how to" resource that you can order from Amazon or anywhere else that walks you through a DIY process of constructing your child. None at all, because let's face it, your child is someone the world has never seen before!

## A Design and a Designated Purpose

But that doesn't mean you're flying blind. No, you have the design of your child to work with, along with their essential presence in this world for this space and time, backing you up as well. So now it comes down to having the immensely fascinating—and, if you let it be, wondrous—journey of walking alongside that little person as they grow and awaken into life. How great is it that *you* get to be there, right beside them, as an integral part of the process!

Make no mistake, in walking beside them you can't help but notice your child's amazing beauty and brilliance, which to you seem so much brighter than they do to anyone else; but also all of their scribbles of imperfection and inadequacy, which appear so much darker and more worrisome to you than to others. All of that is mixed together in the messy middle of every day. Your choice is to trust that you belong there to play your uniquely positioned role in this story that is being written, as only you, the parent, can.

As you see it all unfold, you have to resolutely believe in what you cannot yet see. Remember, you *receive* the child you are given—along with something of a purpose intended not only for your heart and your home, but for such a time as this in our world. Your child is a part of our future. Their unique presence here now is intended to be a gift to the world . . . to all of us. They were born to contribute something of greater significance and meaning, as only they can.

# 2

# you're parenting a person, not a product

Our dad grew up in an era when children were to be "seen and not heard." Not anymore! In many families, children have become the center of gravity for everything else: What the family does and when they do it. What they spend their money on. Where they live. What they eat. Where they vacation. Who their friends are. What feelings are allowed. And so much more.

Honestly, we see families all the time where the kids are running around, doing their own thing—not always for the better. It doesn't take long to start wondering, *Who's in charge here? Where are the parents?*

## The Fear of Parenting

The answer is that in far too many cases, the parents are scared. They're scared they're going to mess up this assignment called parenting. And why wouldn't they? If they themselves are the product of bad parenting, why should they expect to get it right? (That's how they see it, anyway.)

Enter the childrearing "experts." There's a whole industry of them, and they are well aware of parental angst. That's why they've produced no end of blog posts, podcasts, videos, books, manuals, workshops, and websites on the hows and whys of parenting.

But is it at all helpful? Not so much. Much of it is unfiltered. A lot of it uses scare tactics: how to avoid this mistake; why you must *not* do it this way; how some longstanding, well-accepted practice will ruin your kid; why this or that approach is far superior to another. Much of it plays to the is-there-something-wrong-with-my-child? worry that parents so often feel. Not to mention the will-my-child-get-left-out-or-left-behind? angst. And what gets sold as "best practice" by one authority is contradicted by another. Which then divides parents into polarized camps over basic matters such as breastfeeding, potty training, discipline, schooling, chores, working moms vs. stay-at-home moms, healthcare, and on and on.

We're not saying all the advice out there is bad. It's just that there's so much of it. Which only adds to a parent's misgivings: "If it takes this much expertise to raise a child in the right way, what hope is there for me to get it right?"

We hear you loud and clear. Remember, like you, we are both parents. We each brought infants home with the thought, *Now what am I supposed to do?*

## An Approach That Makes Sense

We wish someone had done for us then what we're hoping to do for you now through this book. Rather than hand you a parenting manual, we're going to show you what amounts to an "owner's manual" for *your* child. And like countless parents before you, once you see how that owner's manual works, you're quite likely to say, "This makes so much sense!"

At that point, our bet is that you'll realize the only "right" way to parent your child is to follow that child's owner's manual. Why would you not?

Well, the biggest reason you might not is because of the pre-vailing view of childrearing in our culture, which says that all the burden is on you as a parent to "make" your child into a person. In other words, your child is a product. *Your* product, to be more spe-cific. Your assignment or goal is to turn your newborn (the raw material) into an adult (the finished product). How that child "turns out" (a manufacturing term if ever there was one) at age eighteen or twenty or twenty-two becomes a referendum on how well you as a parent have done the job.

**The prevailing view of childhood in our culture says that all the burden is on you as a parent to "make" your child into a person. In other words, your child is a product.**

That view gets expressed all the time when people say, "I am the way I am today because of my parents." For instance, some-one gets praised for their work ethic. They reply, "Well, that's because my dad was an extremely hard worker who never quit until he finished the job." Or, on the negative side, someone is told they're a perfectionist. They reply, "You're right. I'm so sorry! It's just that I never could live up to my mother's expectations."

In short, countless people walk around assuming that who they are—or rather, who they've "become"—is primarily due to the influ-ence of their parents. It follows, then, that they in turn will be the pri-mary influence on who their kids become. Everyone is the product of their upbringing, right? That's why parents are supposed to raise children the right way, so they turn out right.

Right? Wrong!

## Your Child Is a Person

Without question, parents have a profound influence on their chil-dren, as we'll see. But the flaw with saying a child is a product is that a child is not a product. *A child is a person.* That changes everything!

So what is your purpose as a parent? Instead of trying to "make" your child into someone, your assignment is to nurture the growth of the infant person you have been given you into the adult person they are intended to be. The baby you brought into the world was a person before they ever showed up on the weighing table. Since at least the 1970s, researchers have been studying the remarkable ways in which childhood development begins early on in the womb. By the time of birth, "the newborn infant is both competent and complexly organized."[1]

So said one of the pioneers in this field, the late Dr. T. Berry Brazelton, professor emeritus at Harvard Medical School. He pointed out that "a newborn already has nine months of experience when she is born. She is capable of controlling her behavior in order to respond to her new environment."[2] Moreover, she communicates to others through her behavior, even if not yet through developed language. And she is also a social creature, an individual with her own unique qualities, ready to shape as well as be shaped by her environment.[3]

**Pay close attention to who this new person is telling you they already are.**

Your child is bringing their own unique personhood into your home, which is now their home, too. It's not your job to try and tell them who they should be (that's a hopeless task, by the way). Rather, the better path by far is to *pay close attention to who this new person is telling you they already are.*

We can help you with that, since we're in the business of helping individuals find their "giftedness," what they are born to do.

We're going to tell you much more about giftedness. But right off the bat, here are two game-changing realities you should know about. First, everyone has their own unique form of giftedness. You. Your child. Your spouse (if you're married). Your other children (if you have any). Everyone.

Second, giftedness shows up very, very early in life—so early that it may be inborn, though there's really no way to prove that. But we know it's there early on. At The Giftedness Center, people have told us—in remarkable detail for the age they were at the time—stories about activities they enjoyed doing when they were only four, three, even two and a half years old! And those stories dovetail perfectly with a consistent pattern of behavior they still manifest decades later.

Can you see where we're going? Your child brings you something special wrapped up in who they are: their giftedness. As their parent, it's your privilege (as well as your responsibility, we believe) to begin to look for that giftedness, and in turn help your child begin to see their giftedness and treasure it as something special. Doing so will transform the parenting process for you.

Sound appealing? Then here's where we're headed. . .

## The Layout of This Book

### Part I: *Your Purpose as a Parent*

In the rest of Part I, we're going to lay a foundation by explaining and showing you what giftedness is and what difference it makes for parenting. You and your child form a pair, a dyad, and in that parent-child relationship both of your respective forms of giftedness interact with each other. But because you're the adult and hold most of the power, you have to be especially aware that you live into your role as a parent through the lens of your giftedness.

### Part II: *The Early Years*

Your child's giftedness starts showing up right from birth. We'll show you a simple method you can use to begin discovering it even during their infant, preschool, and early elementary years. That discovery process will continue through their teenage years into adulthood.

### Part III: *Education*

Your child's giftedness profoundly affects how they learn. So in this section we'll help you think through what that means for your child's schooling and how to optimize their learning in elementary, junior high, and high school. We'll also point out ways to use academic and extracurricular activities to make further discoveries about their giftedness.

### Part IV: *The Teenage Years*

With adolescence come some challenging changes in your child's life—which in turn pose challenges for you as a parent. But one thing that won't change is your child's giftedness, and that can become a bedrock on which to help them gain confidence and build a positive self-image. During these years, your child will express their giftedness in far more sophisticated ways, which can help you as a parent start to fill in a lot more of the details in your understanding of their core personhood.

### Part V: *Getting Ready for Liftoff*

As your high schooler moves closer toward graduation, both they and you as the parent are naturally starting to ponder what's next for them. In this section we'll show you how to pull together your acquired observations about your child's giftedness into a summary form that can help them own and lean into their core strengths, and even begin to develop something of a vision for their life in the adult world.

## A Recommendation

Our guess is that you probably want to just flip to the sections of the book that most directly address the age and stage of your child. For example, if you're the parent of a newborn, you're eager to turn to Part II: The Early Years. Or if you've got a twelve-year-old "tween" driving you crazy, you want to go right to Part IV on the teenage years.

That's understandable. But our strong recommendation is to finish Part I first before moving on. Everything from chapter 6 on is based on chapters 1 through 5. By reading them first, you'll have a proper orientation to everything else we have to say.

And we begin with a story about what it looks like when a parent knows nothing about giftedness.

# 3

# the indelible signature of giftedness

Once upon a time there was a hammer named Harry. Harry the Hammer learned from an early age that whenever he hit something, it usually gave way to the force of his energy. Sometimes that turned out okay, sometimes not. But either way, Harry the Hammer found that he loved to hit things. It just felt great!

As hammers tend to do, Harry made a huge impression on others. So as he got older, he became quite popular. People regarded him as a leader. Someone with a future. Someone who was going to make a big impact with his life.

And then Harry the Hammer met Ethel the Eggbeater. It was absolutely love at first sight! It had to be, right, since opposites tend to attract?

So Harry the Hammer and Ethel the Eggbeater married and settled down. Well, not exactly "settled." You see, Ethel was very old-school and very different from her husband. Whereas he liked to nail things down, she liked to stir things up. Needless to say, she created a lot of drama! That often irritated her husband. But at least she made his life interesting. And the sex was, well, incredible!

Which eventually led to a baby—little Larry the Screwdriver. Harry was so proud! At last he had a son. A son who could carry on his name and the Hammer legacy. And for that reason, Harry was bound and determined to raise his little boy right. "I'm going to give him everything my father never gave me," he said to himself. (We forgot to mention that Harry's father was a slide rule.[1] What an embarrassment for a hammer to have a dad like that!)

So Harry began to raise little Larry, and Larry followed Daddy everywhere. One of his earliest memories was sitting in the backyard, watching Daddy use his big, flat head to come down on a nail and knock it into a block of wood. Wow, that was something! Daddy was so strong and powerful! Imagine being able to do that! Like so many boys do, Larry aspired to become just like his daddy and do the same things Daddy could do. Pretty soon he was dressing up like Daddy and pretending to be a little hammer with his friends.

When he got old enough, Larry started hitting real nails. He discovered that was really hard! At least, it was hard for him. To his disappointment, he found he wasn't particularly good at driving nails. And also that whenever he did, it kind of hurt. Like really hurt! But that's what Daddy did, so Larry kept at it.

To his credit, Harry the Hammer hung in there with his struggling son. He spent time coaching him on how to drive nails. In fact, every afternoon after Harry got home from work, he took Larry out to the backyard and brought out the box of nails and a block of wood. They'd practice and practice driving nails, with Harry explaining and demonstrating the technique and Larry doing his best to get the hang of it.

Then when Larry got older, Harry signed him up for a hammering team so his son could be around hammers his own age. That helped somewhat, although Larry spent far too much time on the bench. Also, sometimes when the team lost a game, a couple of the star hammers would complain that Larry had "screwed things up." That really hurt, and Larry resolved to do better. But truth be told, Larry was turning out to be a bit of disappointment, not only to his team but to his father. And also to himself. "I'll never be the hammer my dad is," Larry began telling himself.

And in fact, he never was.

## That Look

Does that story make you feel a bit sad? It should, because the same basic tale plays itself out day after day, year after year, all over this world. Well-intentioned parents are doing their best to raise their children as best they know how. Meanwhile, kids are growing up doing their best to please Mommy or Daddy, but so often they can see That Look in their parent's eyes. That Look of disappointment. Or irritation. Or frustration. Or exasperation. Or maybe even outright anger. Or worse, disgust or contempt. Whatever the feeling, it's That Look that says, "What's wrong with you?"

Sometimes it's more than a look, it's an actual outburst: "What's wrong with you?!" Because that's what we as humans do when someone does things differently than we would do them. When someone goes about a task differently than we would do it; when they make a decision using a different approach than we would; when they fail to take action that we would have taken—our instinctive reaction is to think, or maybe even say, "What's wrong with you?!" It's just human nature.

But of course, there's a simple answer to that question that explains everything. That answer is: There's nothing wrong with the other person. They're just not you!

## "Your Child Is Who They Be"

The task of parenting is never really easy, but it gets a lot easier if a parent can make peace with that simple fact: *Your child is not you.* That may seem obvious, but it's amazing how often a parent can forget that as they interact with their child.

Your child is not you, and that's a wonderful thing! Not that there's anything wrong with you, but what we mean is that your child is not supposed to be you. Indeed, they *cannot* be you—just as you cannot *not* be you. Your child is whoever they are. As a mentor of ours named Gladys Guy Brown used to put it, "Your child is who they be."

By this point you may be thinking: *Okay, I get the point. My child is a different person than I am. I can see that. My child is not me.*

So then, who are they?

In the last chapter we said that your child comes with a kind of "owner's manual" that explains who they are. Have you ever worked on a car or a computer or some other sophisticated piece of equipment? The wise thing to do when you take on a task like that is to check the owner's manual first to find out what that machine was designed to do, what it does best, what it takes to get it to do that, and what other pieces of equipment it needs around it in order to operate the way it was designed to operate. And you'd especially want to pay attention to the Warnings section of that owner's manual, the cautions that say, "Whatever you do with this piece of equipment, *don't* do this!"

Your child's owner's manual is found in their *giftedness,* which means what they are *born* to do. Everybody is born to do something. For one person it's to solve problems. They never met a problem they didn't want to solve. For someone else it's to understand something at a very deep level. For another it's to build or make something and get a finished product. For yet another it's to come up with some imaginative concept in their mind and then create something—perhaps a painting, a song, a story, a sculpture—so that the rest of us can experience that concept. For another, it's simply being part of a group or team and collaborating to get something done.

There are endless forms of giftedness. Indeed, there are as many forms of giftedness as there are human beings, because it turns out that while giftedness is universal, every person has their own unique giftedness. No two people are exactly the same. We each have our own unique personhood.

## Your Own Unique Signature

You can find out more about the nature of giftedness in a previous book that Bill has written entitled *The Person Called You: Why You're Here, Why You Matter & What You Should Do With Your Life*. In that book, Bill defined giftedness like this:

> Giftedness is the unique way in which you function. It's a set of inborn core strengths and natural motivation you instinctively and consistently use to do things that you find satisfying and productive. Giftedness is not just what you can do, but what you are born to do, enjoy doing, and do well.[2]

That takes things a step beyond the analogy of an owner's manual. It means that giftedness is more like your own unique signature. Both your signature and your giftedness uniquely represent you because both uniquely come from you.

To use one of the examples above: You may have giftedness for solving problems, but you will solve problems like no other problem-solver solves problems. You'll be interested in particular kinds of problems, and you'll go about solving them in a particularly distinctive way. That way flows right out of your personhood and who you are, with the result that each problem you solve essentially ends up with your personal signature on it.

And if that's true for you, it's equally true for your child. When they learn to write, they end up writing in a distinctive way, which leads to a distinctive signature. The same is true of their giftedness. As they begin to express that giftedness, it becomes clear that they "do life" in a distinctive way. They "sign" every day, as it were, with their own indelible signature. Your task as a parent is to get to know that signature and then help your child learn to recognize it. You want them to start seeing the kinds of things in this world that "have their name on it," so to speak. We'll show you how to do that beginning in Part II.

## What Giftedness Is Not

Just to be clear, by "giftedness" we do *not* mean:

- *unusual talent.* People talk about "gifted" athletes or "gifted musicians" or others with seemingly outsized abilities. It's as if giftedness is for the favored few. But in fact, giftedness is universal. Every human being has their own form of giftedness, whether or not it looks spectacular to others. All giftedness has intrinsic value and is given for a purpose.

- *Talented and Gifted (TAG) programs* or "gifted and talented education" (GATE or G/T) in the schools. We're not opposed to those programs, but again, all children have their own unique form of giftedness. And yes, it affects their learning, as we will see.

- *an occupational title.* Giftedness is not in the work one does, but in the person doing the work. Someone who is born to solve problems can express that giftedness through any number of occupations.

Again, *The Person Called You* can give you the lowdown on all the ins and outs of giftedness. Our concern here is, what difference does giftedness make for parenting? The next chapter will begin to answer that question by pointing out five things you need to know as a parent when it comes to giftedness.

# 4

..................

# five things
# parents need
# to know

Your child is a person with their own unique giftedness, and that affects everything about your role as a parent. To be specific, here are five things you need to be aware of:

1. Your child's giftedness shows up early.

2. Your child's giftedness reveals itself through a pattern of motivated behavior.

3. Your child's giftedness is unique to your child.

4. The more you discover your child's giftedness and honor it, the more loved your child will feel and the healthier and more confident they will be.

5. The cost of ignoring your child's giftedness—or worse, blocking, shaming, or wounding it—can be severe.

Let's take these in turn.

### 1. Your Child's Giftedness Shows Up Early

How early? Right from birth, some say. But regardless, very early on, as an infant grows beyond the sleep-cry-nurse-poop stage, they start noticing, engaging, and interacting with their world. That activity initially seems random and spontaneous. But give it some time, and things begin to coalesce into some signature ways that your little person reaches out to their world and responds to it.

Your child's giftedness shows up early—and that's good news! For one thing, it takes a lot of pressure off you as a parent to realize that you don't have to "make" your child into somebody, because they already *are* somebody. What's more, it means you've got something to work with as you think about how to rear *this* particular child. You've got their giftedness. You don't know yet what it is, but you will soon because we're going to help you begin discovering it.

Remember Harry the Hammer? Harry didn't know anything about giftedness. He didn't know there is such a thing as giftedness, and he only had a vague, rudimentary sense of his own giftedness. So in raising Larry the Screwdriver, he did what most parents do: he raised him according to what made sense to Harry. But that didn't fit Larry. And "fit" is really important.

The first lesson in raising a child is to *use an approach that fits the child*. That requires paying attention to their giftedness.

### 2. Your Child's Giftedness Reveals Itself Through a Pattern of Motivated Behavior

Giftedness is part of your child's core personhood, or identity, which expresses itself through your child's behavior. Especially *motivated behavior*. What does that mean?

If you've got a toddler or preschooler, the next time you take them to a playground and let them run around, sit back and just watch what different children are choosing to do. Over there is a group sliding down the slide, over and over, squealing with delight, chasing each other to get to the ladder first, laughing at each other's antics, an absolute circus of excitement, reveling in one another.

Nearby are two little ones absorbed with a swing. For a while, one pushes harder and harder and the other swings higher and higher. Then they stop and trade places. Over and over. Time slips by, unnoticed.

In a solitary sandbox is a boy building his own imaginative world. It's not just sand he's looking at. It's a castle and a domain, with a king and his army, and an invading enemy to be defended against. And over there is the lair of a hideous dragon! The scene is absolutely real in the boy's mind for that moment. Indeed, it would be accurate to say he is "lost in his own little world."

**Too often we turn difference into a problem.**

And let's not overlook the five-ish-looking girl flopped on the ground near the bench where you are sitting with her parent, chatting. The girl doesn't appear to be at all bored or tired. But she just sits and says nothing. And something suggests she is keen to stick close to her parent and not engage with the other children if she doesn't have to.

Now why do you suppose that is?

### Observing, not explaining

Hold on! See how instinctive it is to ask that *why* question? So often when we take note of something (or someone) "different," we are inclined to ask why? Nothing wrong with that, except that all too often we then turn the difference into a problem. We start psychologizing the child's behavior and describing the child in terms of a perceived "pathology."

For that reason, *why* is the absolute wrong question for a parent to ask. Indeed, *why* turns out to be one of the major reasons parents so often don't "get" their children. When one goes down the *why* trail of speculation, they end up trying to explain their child's behavior instead of just observing it.

But guess what? Your child does not want you to explain them. They want you to *notice* them—not passively, but actively. They want you to let *them* show you who they are. To let them be that person. And to appreciate and value "who that person be."

When you start asking *why*, you are on the verge of asking that most terrible of relational questions: "What's wrong with you?!"

Okay, back to the playground. In the case of the quiet girl, there's nothing wrong with her, as anyone who has paid attention to her over time would know. They would have noticed that she likes to come to the park and sit and watch things and make up rhymes in her head that she takes home and recites to her family at dinner. It's just something she likes to do. She has found that playing with the other children interferes with that satisfying activity, and so she chooses to remain aloof rather than engage in all their play. And yes, she has found that there's something comforting and relaxing about being near her parent—that particular parent—something that actually stimulates her to go inside her mind to that happy place where she makes up rhymes.

### Motivated behavior

Now what we've just illustrated at the playground is *motivated behavior*. That means behaving in a particular way where *the person* gets to choose the activity and how they want to do it. So we see that some kids like to be part of a bigger group. Others like to pare the group down to just two of them. Other children quite honestly prefer to be alone a lot. One might enjoy building something. Another enjoys the sounds of words and what can be done with them when she puts those sounds together.

Yes, this is all simple behavior. As these children grow into teens and then adults, their motivated behavior will become far more sophisticated. But the point is, the behavior comes out of the children themselves. No one is forcing them to play together or play by themselves, to climb or swing as opposed to making something, to forget about Mommy or Daddy, or to stick close to home. The motivation comes from within and expresses itself through *chosen behavior that feels satisfying* in some way to each child.

**Behavior that is satisfying tends to get repeated.**

Behavior that feels satisfying tends to get repeated. As the child grows it gets repeated enough to where it becomes a pattern in the child's life.

For example, one of the girls who loves to go up and down the slide with the parade of other children begins to show a pattern of preferring group activities. At school she befriends lots of other children. She gets excited about group-oriented activities like plays and group sings and rallies in the gym. She eventually joins a soccer team and thrives in the camaraderie of a shared effort. She excels in classes where students are organized to work on group projects, and people experience her collaborative style as a sort of glue that holds teams together.

Meanwhile, the boy in the sandbox, lost in his own little world, has a place at home that is all his own. He spends countless hours there by himself, happily building LEGO projects, assembling models, and putting together and flying Estes Rockets. He also reads anything he can find on explorers, adventurers, heroes, and historical figures. It's a fascinating pattern of admiration for people who accomplished great things, mixed with an inquisitive curiosity to find out how things work.

And what about the girl who loves rhymes? As soon as she learns to write, she starts collecting her verses in homemade books that she illustrates and then adds to her own library. Then one day her second-grade teacher discovers that this girl has a lovely voice, and she asks her to sing a brief solo in a class production. She does, and her moment in the spotlight is a hit with the audience. So her folks make what, for them, is a real financial sacrifice and begin paying for voice lessons. That leads to getting parts in musicals in high school. On the side, the girl picks up the guitar and starts composing and performing her own songs. She turns out to be an excellent student in all of her courses, but everyone knows she is most alive whenever she opens her mouth to sing.

Giftedness is seen in a pattern of behavior that is consistent and unchanging over time. Children come back to activities that prove satisfying—meaning, satisfying *to them*. That makes perfect sense. No one cares to repeat behavior that they find boring, pointless, painful, or something they can't stand.

No, for each of us as persons there are certain activities that stimulate our energies and hold our attention until we are able to fulfill some core satisfaction that only we experience. We repeat those activities—or activities like them—because of course we want to gain that satisfaction over and over again. That's as true for children on a playground as it is for adults in the grown-up world. That's the nature of giftedness.

Which is why we're going to help you as a parent watch for signs of your child's giftedness. You have to intentionally be on the lookout for it because no two children's giftedness is exactly the same.

### 3. Your Child's Giftedness Is Unique to Your Child

This is another piece of good news for you as a parent! Somewhere along the way the idea took hold that there's some "normal" way that children are supposed to behave, and there's something "wrong" with the child who acts differently from that standard. Like the girl in the scene above, sitting near her parent instead of playing with the other children. "What's wrong with her?!"

You know how this works, don't you? "Everyone knows" that (all) children love to play on playgrounds. They (all) like candy. They (all) want to be around other kids their age. They (all) eventually want to play sports. They (all) want to win. They (all) enjoy creativity. They (all) need to be told what to do. They (all) enjoy games. They (all) like to make as much noise as they can. They (all) like to run around and get their energy out. They (all) should play a musical instrument. They (all) need teachers in order to learn. They (all) need to learn to be leaders. They (all) are motivated to behave in ways that will earn them a reward.

No.

Not so.

While children indeed share much in common and often display similar kinds of behavior, each one is unique when it comes to their own motivated behavior, or giftedness. Which means that if your child prefers an activity that seems different from the activity "all the other children" are doing, that's okay. Your job is to get in tune with your child and hear the unique "music" only they can make, not compare them to the other children and conclude there must be something wrong with your child.

Let's be clear: we're not talking about behavioral disorders or behavior that is deviant or maladaptive in ways that could or do cause harm, either to the child or others. Any sort of disruptive behavior from your child that concerns you warrants careful evaluation by medical or psychological professionals to assess any issues that require attention. If needed, they can provide the appropriate support measures and treatment options to help your child.

But when we talk about giftedness, we're talking about behavior that is positive and healthy, that captures a child's focus and brings out the best of their energies, that brings them—and oftentimes others—joy or satisfaction or delight. We're talking about their wonder—what makes them wonderful or filled with wonder. That behavior may seem unusual or surprising to a parent because it looks different or is just unexpected. But in fact, behavior that seems out of the ordinary is sometimes the parent's best clue that they are looking at an expression of their child's giftedness.

### *The angel food cake*

For example, when Bill was about five years old, our mom informed him that she had to be away for the afternoon. So he asked what he should do while she was gone (Billy and boredom were never a good combination). Mom thought for a moment and said, "Well, tonight we're going to celebrate Daddy's birthday, and he wants an angel food cake. So you can mix up the cake ingredients and bake them in the oven while I'm gone. Then we can put the icing on the cake when I get back." (Mom knew that Billy was already well acquainted with how to put the milk and eggs in the cake mix and stir it all up, and then pour the mix into the pan, and how to set the oven.)

Several hours later, when Mom returned home, the house smelled like a bakery! Mom looked in on Billy, who was in his room playing, and then went to the kitchen. But a minute or so later she was back— wearing a puzzled look as she held an unopened box of Duncan Hines Angel Food Cake Mix.

"How did you bake the cake without using this cake mix?"

"I used the recipe in your cookbook," Billy replied.

And so he had. He had pulled down our mom's worn copy of *The Woman's Home Companion Cookbook*, looked up the recipe for angel food cake, gotten out all the ingredients, measured them into a bowl, separated the egg whites and whipped them with a mixer until they were firm, added the wet ingredients to the dry, folded in the egg whites, coated the angel food pan with butter and a dusting of flour, poured in the batter, set the oven, baked the cake, pulled it out when done, and then flipped the pan over and set it on a Coke bottle to cool.

Not exactly what one would expect from a five-year-old, was it?

Separating eggs and folding egg whites, let alone smoothly getting an "upside down" cake out of a pan, is tricky even for an experienced cook. But then, Billy never was a typical kid at any age, and the record does show that he absolutely did it, and he enjoyed doing it, and the cake turned out great.

By this point you may be wondering, *So did that turn out to be Bill's giftedness, to bake cakes?* The answer is: it doesn't work that way. The giftedness is not in the activity; it's in the person. Baking that cake was merely one activity that expressed *how* Bill goes about anything that matters to him. If we looked at more of his stories, we would see that same approach, but expressed in other ways. For the record, though, Bill still loves to cook—and it brings great joy, not only to him but to all the people around him!

Not all expressions of giftedness are unusual or spectacular. Indeed, most are really not. Giftedness is usually seen in very mundane, everyday activities. Things like how a person learned to ride a bike, or how someone painted a picture for an elementary school project, or how a boy loved to use an edger on the family lawn, or how someone sold more Girl Scout cookies than her fellow Girl Scouts.

The activity may be very simple, but what is always present is an energy, a focus, an engagement with the activity. The child comes alive when pursuing motivated behavior. What may have looked ordinary actually becomes quite extraordinary when we see the "light in their eyes" that tells us the activity has flipped a switch in them. That's how we discover what the giftedness is. We remain on the lookout for that enthusiasm, that light, that energy.

## 4. The More You Discover Your Child's Giftedness and Honor It, the More Loved Your Child Will Feel and the Healthier and More Confident They Will Be

We indicated earlier that your child's giftedness is the key to their personhood and who they are—"who they be." By expressing their giftedness, your child is telling you and the rest of the world what makes them special, what makes them a gift to the world. As the parent, you have the awesome privilege of starting to unwrap that gift and behold who it is and honor that person your child was born to be.

But what does that mean, to "honor" your child's giftedness? Three things, at least:

### Notice it.

Too many parents are passive in their parenting, and for that reason they are, as the theatrical Hamilton would say, "throwing away their shot."[1] It doesn't matter whether they think their child will "turn out" just fine (whatever that means). They will have missed their moment every bit as much as a farmer will be almost guaranteed to fail at farming if he has spent every day of the growing season on the porch, watching TV. At harvest time, there may somehow be a few ears of corn to pick, and that's "fine." But no thanks to the farmer!

**Too many parents are passive in their parenting.**

Parenting requires intentionality because what are the odds that a child can figure out how to grow up and be who they are on their own? Especially when the outside world is standing ready to squeeze each of us into its mold. You are there as the perfect person for that all-important job because you're the one they trust with all their heart. What's more, because of the work we do, we can tell you that we've never seen anyone who could completely figure out their giftedness solely on their own. Giftedness gets revealed over time through interaction with others in the world. That's why parents have such a strategic role to play: they are the first audience to whom the little person they have brought into the world will perform the daily scenes that, over time, reveal their unique story of giftedness. Who would want to miss that?

So first of all, notice your child's giftedness. Then. . .

### Celebrate it.

Have you ever knocked yourself out to buy someone the "perfect" gift? You spent hours and days mulling over what they'd really like. At last you settled on what to give them. *That's it!* you thought to yourself. *They'll love it!* So you went about getting that gift—maybe by saving up some money, or hunting all over town or the internet to find it, or maybe spending hours making it yourself. At last you got it ready. Then you figured out how to present it to them: the right time, the right setting, the right packaging, the right reveal. At last the moment came, and you gave them the gift!

And they said, "Oh." (Pause.) "That's nice."

How did that feel?

"That's nice" is not as bad a reaction as That Look. But it's not much better.

Now you're probably thinking we're getting ready to give the talk on praise and affirmation. You know, the one where you're told that children especially need to be affirmed because not doing so will hurt their self-esteem. So go out of your way to make a big deal out of any and every picture they draw, thing they make, story they write, assignment they complete . . . No matter how lame, poorly executed, or downright awful the finished product is, at least give them applause and a trophy for their effort. In other words: tell your child they are great at things, and eventually they will believe it, and that will help them gain a positive self-image. Surely you've heard that message because it's become wildly popular in recent years.

Well, that is not our message. Our message is surprisingly different:

When your child lets you know about something that has mattered to them, *stop and notice it.* Then say, "Tell me more about that." And just listen to whatever they have to say.

If you listen carefully, you'll find that they're not initially asking you to evaluate (or judge or give a grade to) whatever it is they have done. They just want you to *see* it. Which is virtually the same as saying they want you to see *them.* To see what interests them, what they cared about enough to devote time and some energy to. What they are able (or becoming able) to do. What they take satisfaction in.

By noticing, you open a door into celebrating what they have brought you. For what they have brought you is their giftedness. They would never call it that. They don't even know what giftedness is (yet). But they've brought an expression to you right out of their giftedness.

So yes, maybe you remark about whatever thing they have brought: "Wow, I like that color," or "Honey, I had no idea you could do that," or "This is even better than the last one!"

But the celebrating is about them as a person. You can do that by simply saying something like, "Wow, you really seem to enjoy putting all those pieces together!" Or "I was wondering what you were doing in your room all that time. Now I can see you really were working hard." Or "I love it when you draw flowers and things like that. In fact, I'm going to put that picture right here on the refrigerator so it can remind me of you every time I see the flowers you drew for me!"

Your child is not so much looking for you to tell them they've done a "good job" when they show you some expression of their giftedness; rather, they want to know that you value them for being who they were born to be and doing what they were born to do. Their show-and-tell gives you an opportunity to do that. And children who are valued for who they were born to be and do can't help but feel loved, as well as grow in their self-confidence.

So first, notice your child's giftedness. Then celebrate it. Then. . .

### Go with it.

In other words, work with your child's giftedness. Cooperate with it. Give it opportunity.

Tonya was raised by a single mother who earned her living as a ballet teacher. That means Tonya grew up at the ballet studio. Not surprisingly, it also means she began learning to dance at an early age.

Tonya noticed that at the end of the day's lessons, there was always a lot to do in cleaning up the studio and getting it ready for the next day. So Tonya was expected to help put things in order while her mother sat down to work on the scheduling and the books before the two of them would go home for dinner. But Tonya didn't mind doing that. In fact, she actually enjoyed it. She liked having responsibility. And she liked being able to help her mother. It didn't take long for Tonya's mother to see that. She was very, very appreciative for her daughter's help.

So when Tonya asked if she could start helping with the scheduling, her mother (wisely) said yes. She showed her how and where to put the entries into the calendar. Before long, Tonya was not only entering data, she was answering the phone and making arrangements for lessons with students and parents.

In her early teens, Tonya started looking over the books while her mother was teaching lessons. Math was one of her better subjects in school, and she couldn't help but notice that sometimes her mom would make mistakes in how she added up the numbers. It wasn't that her mom was poor at arithmetic. It's just that by the end of the day she was exhausted, and she was trying to keep the books when her mind was not clear. So Tonya asked her mother if she could take over the bookkeeping. That would be a big responsibility! But since Tonya had acquitted herself well in all her other duties, her mom (wisely) said yes.

Can you see where this was going? Whether out of prudence or out of simple necessity, Tonya's mother was giving her daughter opportunities to express her giftedness at higher and higher levels. As a result, Tonya grew and developed in taking responsibility in more sophisticated ways.

And her confidence grew, as well. Not so much through the appreciation of her mother—though there was nothing wrong with that—but through her own proven competence. Tonya came to know what she was capable of doing. She was becoming very confident that she could learn whatever she needed to learn in order to take on a responsibility that met a practical need. Tonya was discovering her giftedness and learning to exercise it with authority. Tonya and her mother are a great example of how honoring a child's giftedness is supposed to work.

## 5. The Cost of Ignoring Your Child's Giftedness—or Worse, Blocking, Shaming, or Wounding It—Can Be Severe

Our work is based on the powerful truth that every human is intended to be a gift to the world. Each person has been given something to contribute that can help the world and its people flourish. As specialists in this area, we not only believe that with both of our respective hearts, we've seen that reality borne out over and over in the lives of the people we've worked with.

So how is it that so many children grow up to feel worthless and empty and without direction or purpose? Perhaps because they've never been noticed. Or, to be more specific, their giftedness has never been brought to light. Nor has it been celebrated, let alone given opportunity.

Again, let's go back to Larry the Screwdriver. That parable ends in sadness because Larry was never noticed. Meaning, the thing he did best was never noticed. What was that thing? Well, to turn screws, obviously.

Obvious to you and us, of course, but not to his parents. Why not? Probably because they dismissed it when they did see it, since they didn't realize what they were looking at. Probably because the father in particular had a script already written for who Larry was "supposed" to be. And quite possibly because when they did see Larry turning screws, they disparaged that activity as "wrong," as off script, as distracting from "what really matters."

### *"He's not going to get anywhere!"*

Perhaps you think we're being simplistic or even silly by using Larry the Screwdriver to try and explain something as complex as parenting. But there's nothing simplistic about Jonathan the cello player, whose only real desire in life has been to find the secret of making his instrument produce the perfect sound, so as to penetrate into the very soul of anyone who hears it.

But his father, Vince, the mega-successful plaintiff's attorney, is completely disappointed in his son. Vince is what you might call a "powerful" man. Supremely confident. Self-made. Decisive. Built to win. For Vince, life is about winning the contest. Coming out on top. That credo has served him pretty well in his chosen career. And it has provided a really nice lifestyle for his family.

But now Vince's son says he wants to walk away from all that and try his luck as a musician. How insane is that? How risky can he be in a world where symphony orchestras are collapsing like folding chairs? And that's if he even gets a job! Vince just doesn't know what to make of all this.

Nor does Jonathan. All Jonathan sees from his father is That Look. He still hasn't figured out what it means exactly. Disappointment, for sure. But maybe also irritation? Anger? Perhaps even contempt?

Whatever That Look from his father means, it certainly doesn't say, "Wow, Jonathan, you really enjoy making your cello sing, don't you? That's a wonderful thing! I love it when you can get it to do that. That cello brings out the best in you."

We have seen this scenario play out again and again. Parents not "getting" their children, simply missing who they are as persons. It's like ships passing in the night. So caught up in what matters to them, the parents pay no attention to what matters to their children—nor what matters *about* their children.

What matters to Vince is the win, the score, the kill (Vince flew fighter jets in the military). He looks at his son and thinks, *That boy is not going to get anywhere! He doesn't have any goals! All he wants to do is sit around and play his cello.*

But what Vince doesn't see is that his son is not *trying* to "get anywhere"! That's not what he's about. Unlike his father, he wasn't born to do life by goals. He was born to make sounds. To create moods. To tell stories through music. To sail beneath and beyond the towering bridges of logic and reason into the far more nuanced but no less powerful deeps of the soul.

Notice that, Vince! Pay attention to that! Jonathan is showing you his very *being*. Don't take that away from him. Don't shame it just because it's not you. Let it express itself. It's Jonathan's gift to the world. Quite frankly, it's one thing you *can't* do because you're not wired to do it. But he is. So let him be who is and express who he is through what he does best.

### *The dire consequences of unconscious parenting*

The alternative is . . . well, let's just say it almost never turns out well. We're not psychologists, but in our work we often hear stories that go all the way back into early childhood and up through the elementary, adolescent, and teen years. Our primary focus is on the storyteller and what they did, but it's interesting how much the storyteller sometimes reveals about their parents. As Mom or Dad appear in the stories, we can't help but read between the lines.

In the "best" cases, you might say, the person's parents were enthusiastically behind them all the way, cheering them on. By good fortune, the parents recognized the potential in their son or daughter and wholeheartedly supported them in pursuing activities and paths that fit them. We also frequently hear about (and sometimes even get to meet) parents who never really "got" their child, but made peace with that by being wise enough to realize their child was simply different than they were. And so they, too, generally supported their child as they made decisions and found their path in life.

But then we've also worked with people whose parents treated them with what might be called "benign neglect." The parents weren't against the child. But then they weren't really for them, either. In truth the parents weren't really there. Oh, they were there physically, but they were passive, not really noticing their son or daughter, let alone noticing their giftedness. For eighteen or more years their child gave them plenty of clues to work with. But with most all of those clues, the reaction was just, "Oh." (Pause.) "That's nice."

The saddest cases we see are where some real damage has been done—often, mind you, by well-intentioned parents. We're not describing bad people (for the most part). We're describing good people who unintentionally did some really bad parenting.

For example, they shamed their child's gift by describing it—sometimes "kiddingly"—using a negative label: "OCD," "control freak," "dreamer," "picky," "brainiac," "Miss Bossy Pants," "ADD," "out in left field," "center stage," "nerd," "here comes Trouble!" "jack of all trades, master of none." We could go on and on. For just about every kind of giftedness we've seen, someone has come up with a pejorative label for it.

When your parent gives you feedback about something that is undeniably true about you, but wraps that message in a nasty label that is negative and humiliating, they sear into your soul a sense of shame that you may never get free of. And because it's your powerful and beloved parent that is saying it, that label is something you will always remember and internalize in the deepest part of who you are. Because, you cannot *not* do that thing that you do, your giftedness. But from then on, every time you do it, you hear your parent's voice pronouncing that label over your gift, belittling that thing that brings you joy, thereby tainting your joy with shame and pain. "Oops! There I go again, being a perfectionist" (or control freak, or know-it-all, or troublemaker, or whatever). "I'll never be able to change!" And sadly, you may never know that you are actually trying to live out some of the *best* of who you are.

### Punished for being himself

Some parents actually punish their children for exercising their gifts. More often than not, they are doing so out of love and good intentions—sadly misguided, however. That's because parents tend to affirm in their kids what they, the parents, perceive as valuable. They want their kids to act according to what makes sense to them, by virtue of their own giftedness. So when they see their child doing something they regard as praiseworthy, they lavish all kind of kudos on them for that behavior. But when the child expresses a strength that the parent doesn't recognize as advantageous or worthy, or that somehow offends their core values, they are likely to punish or shame the child (and the gift).

Ronny is a case in point. Ronny was born to be part of a team, to play his special role on a team. Groups and teams make sense to him. He is never so happy as when he can participate on a team and contribute to the team's efforts.

Unfortunately, Ronny was born into a family where the father happens to be a rugged individualist—a self-made, independent, pull-yourself-up-by-your-own-bootstraps sort of man. Everything of consequence that Ronny's father has ever done, he has done by himself, using his own wits, pluck, and bucks.

It's easy to see the train wreck that is destined to happen in that father-son relationship. On the one side is little Ronny, who just wants to join a team. And whose team do you suppose he wants to join more than any other team in the world? Why, Daddy's team, of course! And so, again and again, Ronny keeps trying to join up with Daddy. But Daddy, with all the best intentions, keeps pushing Ronny away, saying, "Son, you're never going to get anywhere in life unless you learn how to stand on your own two feet! You've got to be able to do things for yourself, you hear? Nobody's going to do it for you. You've got to be self-reliant, able to hold your own. That's what a man does!"

Imagine that scenario playing itself out thousands of times over Ronny's first eighteen years of life. What do you suppose the impact of that rejection will be on Ronny?

## A Disclaimer

In describing what happens when parents don't cooperate with their children's giftedness, we never want to lose sight of the fact that human beings are exceedingly complex creatures. Giftedness explains some very important things, but it by no means explains everything. Human behavior is always affected by countless factors—physiological, biological, chemical, nutritional, psychological, relational, sociological, cultural, environmental, spiritual, and many more.

In this book we are focusing on giftedness. But in explaining human beings, we must always leave the door open to the contribution of additional factors.

# it starts with you

Perhaps the most basic childhood game ever invented is Follow the Leader. It's a pretty simple group game: one person is chosen "leader," then everyone else lines up behind the leader and imitates whatever they do and follows wherever they go.

You know what? The first game of Follow the Leader your child will ever play is with you as a parent. You're the Leader! You decide where to go (at least in the early years). You initiate the behaviors that are to be mimicked. What's more, you set the tone for your child as to what matters in the world and what should be valued.

In this book we talk about valuing your child by paying attention to their giftedness. We've said that affects everything in parenting. But there's a catch! The simple rule of Follow the Leader suggests that before you start trying to see your child's giftedness, you must first see your own.

## what is *your* giftedness?

If your answer to that question is, "I have no clue," then take heart! You're in good company. The fact is, most people don't really know what their giftedness is, certainly not with any clarity or confidence. They probably know bits and pieces of it and have a vague sense of what they "like" to do, or maybe even what they have a "knack" for. But if you asked them point-blank what their giftedness is—what they are born to do—most people would not be able to answer.

Of course, there's another way people respond to the question,

*What is your giftedness?* Thanks to the endless tests, quizzes, questionnaires, and inventories that the assessment industry keeps churning out, many people think we're asking them to tell us what "type" of person they are. "Oh, I'm an INTJ" (Myers-Briggs). "I'm a high D" (DISC). "I'm an Ideation-Maximizer-Futuristic-Woo, and supposedly an Achiever, too, although I'm pretty sure I'm more of an Activator" (StrengthsFinder). Or, if you're under thirty-five (as of the time we are writing this book), "I'm like totally a 7 with a 6 wing and the shadow of anxiety" (Enneagram).

That's not exactly what we mean by giftedness. "Type" is a category, a box if you will, where groups of people who seem to have similar characteristics (or traits) are lumped together. When we talk about giftedness, we're not interested in how you are "like" other people. We want to know what distinguishes you from other people. What makes you unique?

## discovering your giftedness

How do we find that out? Through your story.

As previously mentioned, our work is based on having you tell us certain kinds of stories from your life. Then we look for a pattern of behavior among those stories to discover your giftedness. That's it! That's the basic process: find a partner, tell them your stories, then together look for a pattern.

We use a rather advanced, proprietary methodology for doing that at The Giftedness Center, one designed to produce a detailed, comprehensive, and precise description of a person's giftedness.[1] But anyone can tell stories and look for patterns, and they will discover something about their giftedness. At least, they will if they trust the process and follow some basic but tried-and-true steps.

You can find those steps on a page at our website called

Discovering Your Giftedness: A Step-by-Step Guide.[2]

*We can't stress enough how important it is for you to discover as much as you can about your own giftedness!* Here are five reasons why:

(1) You will gain significant insight into your own strengths, which will not only boost your confidence, but also lead to greater clarity about your purpose and direction in life.

(2) You will gain additional insight into the ways your own parents did or did not recognize and honor your giftedness, and what that felt like as a child, as well as the lingering effects of that for you now.

(3) You will acquire a firsthand understanding of what this giftedness-thing is that you're supposed to discover in your child.

(4) You'll have a basis for comparing and contrasting ways in which your child is like you and different from you.

(5) Someday when you're telling your child about their giftedness, they're going to ask, "So what's your giftedness?" You don't want to be caught saying, "I don't really know!"

# 5

# nurturing the heart of your child

Your giftedness is a big deal not only because it reveals your own inherent uniqueness but because it personalizes what that uniqueness will mean for you as a parent. Every parent's giftedness will dramatically affect how they raise their child.

## Meet Jaimie

Consider Jaimie as a case in point. Jaimie was born to meet challenges. She's been tackling challenges ever since she was a little girl, trying and succeeding at the challenge of keeping up with her older brother and sisters. In fifth grade she trained, competed, and won track events against sixth and even seventh graders. As a high school junior she rose to the challenge of coming back from a torn ACL to lead her basketball team to a regional championship. As a twenty-four-year-old officer in the military, she led her squadron in defending a position in Mosul, Iraq, for thirty-four hours during a hellacious battle until US forces were able to break through and rescue her unit. Out of the twenty-three soldiers under her command, only two were wounded and none was killed.

After leaving the service, Jaimie married, and fourteen months later she gave birth to a little princess of her own, whom she named Danice.

Now how do you suppose Jaimie would approach the task of parenting? With fear and trepidation? Feeling inadequate and overwhelmed? Hardly. Everything in her history predicted that she would see her daughter and her daughter's world through the lens of *challenge*.

That particular motivation can be a decided advantage to a parent. It was for Jaimie, because Danice turned out to be a colicky baby. That drove her father nuts! But Jaimie took it on as a challenge. First she tried everything that her mothering instincts suggested—to no avail. So she stiffened her resolve and plunged into an exhaustive research survey from any and every source: books, articles, podcasts, Google threads, phone calls to neonatologists, pediatricians, and other specialists, even a visit to an obscure homeopathic clinic specializing in feeding issues.

Like so many challenges before this one, Jaimie could feel herself slowly but surely vectoring toward victory. But the final piece remained elusive. Which means she kept digging. And then she hit pay dirt.

For years, Jaimie had experienced migraine headaches. Now, with the stress of a wailing baby, sleepless nights, and the growing irritation of her husband over the whole situation, she found herself once again experiencing migraines. Fighting, as always, for insight and answers, Jaimie happened across some research connecting migraines and a condition called "infantile colic." She learned that mothers who experience migraines are two and a half times more likely to have a colicky baby than mothers who don't get migraines, and that the colic may itself be an early manifestation of migraines in the child. The research went on to suggest that a parent might be able to calm the child by doing the kinds of things that help alleviate the parent's migraines.

Armed with that nugget of wisdom, Jaimie immediately dimmed the lighting in Danice's surroundings and also talked her husband into finding a new home for Thanos, the family's Chihuahua, whose yapping, mingled with the baby's crying, felt like nails being driven through her eardrums.

Within twenty-four hours of those changes, Danice was down to merely whimpering. Twelve hours later she was fast asleep and remained that way for six hours—the longest she had slept since Jaimie had brought her home from the hospital. Getting out of bed the next morning, Jaimie pumped her fists into the air, silently screaming, "Yes!!"

Countless other incidents in Danice's life benefited from her mother's determination to meet challenges: finding a workaround to a childhood allergy; getting Danice moved to a different class with a different teacher after her original teacher proved unresponsive to a problem with bullying; convincing a private school to admit Danice in eighth grade, even though her admission scores were not impressive; and imparting confidence and security to her daughter that they were going to be just fine after Jaimie's husband moved out of the house one day and filed for divorce. Jamie had an amazing knack for finding a way—willing a way—to come out on top.

## Missing the "Good Truth"

Were there any ways in which Jaimie's giftedness created problems for Danice? Yes indeed. Quite a few, actually. But one incident pretty much tells the story. It began when Danice brought home a report card in third grade. In the notes section on the back, Danice's teacher, Mrs. Knowlton, had written, "I have observed that Danice is a shy child, and for that reason I have purposely chosen to not put her in front of the class very much or to take any leadership roles."

*Time out!* If we had our way, the word "shy" would never be used to characterize anyone. In our culture, "shy" almost always implies something negative. One online dictionary defines "shy" as "easily frightened; disposed to avoid a person or thing; hesitant in committing oneself; sensitively diffident or retiring"[1] By those terms, "shy" means there's something wrong with a person.

Suppose we told you that Danice turns out to be the girl at the playground (chapter 4) who enjoyed making up rhymes in her head.

**In our culture, "shy" almost always implies something negative.**

Yes, the girl who simply liked to sit and watch. Was she shy? No! Rather, she was observant. And creative. And clever. And happy. Not "wrong."

Unfortunately, Mrs. Knowlton hadn't seen that good truth about Danice. She probably didn't know how to pay attention to her giftedness. She just cursorily classified her as one of "the quiet ones" in the class. And jumping to a conclusion, she reported the girl to her mother as shy.

The instant Jaimie read "shy" on Danice's report card, she was outraged. She immediately called for a teacher-parent meeting with Mrs. Knowlton to discuss the situation. She let Mrs. Knowlton know in no uncertain terms that it was unacceptable to hold Danice back from situations that she obviously needed go through in order to "force" her to overcome her "shyness." Jaimie believed her daughter just needed opportunities to practice the skills that would make her confident, assertive, eloquent, and leaderly (all traits that Jaimie possessed in abundance).

Mrs. Knowlton assured her she would "work on" Danice. (How could she not, with Jaimie having put the fear of God in her?) "I'm so glad we understand each other," Jaimie said as she stood up to leave, "because no daughter of mine is ever going to be shy!"

That was hardly the end of the matter. Indeed, it was only the beginning, because Jaimie did what Jaimie's giftedness inclined her to do: she received that news that Danice was "shy" as a new challenge.

That new challenge was to "change Danice." To help her go from being "shy" to "not shy." Or better yet, to whatever the opposite of "shy" is (in Jaimie's perception).

## Wanting What's "Best" for Your Child

To be fair, Jaimie just wanted the best for her daughter. And what responsible, respectable parent doesn't want the best for their child? That's the parent's intention, anyway. But Jaimie's parenting of Danice illustrates a sobering reality: oftentimes what makes all the sense in the world to the parent (by virtue of the parent's giftedness) is not necessarily "best" for the child (by virtue of the child's giftedness).

No, if you truly want the *best* for your child, then you have to know your child, so as to know what "best" means *for them*, in light of how *they* are designed.

In simple terms: you need to know your own giftedness, and you need to know your child's giftedness. Earlier we urged you to take advantage of a process we offer for starting to discover your own giftedness. We'll spend the rest of the book helping you learn a simple method for discovering your child's giftedness.

If Jaimie had had that dual insight into who she is and who Danice is, she would have stopped trying to change Danice and instead started championing Danice's personhood. Instead of telling Mrs. Knowlton to put Danice in situations that would force her "not to be shy," she would have become Danice's advocate with the teacher. She might have explained that, "Actually, Danice is not shy at all. She's definitely quiet, but that's because she's absorbed in observing her world and all that is going on around her. Asking her to suddenly be the leader in a group exercise will never work, because she wouldn't have time to prepare and get comfortable. But if you asked her to describe your classroom in a story, or better yet in a poem, I think you'd be amazed at what she'd come up with!"

## The Way of the Child

This idea of raising a child based on who the child turns out to be is hardly new. Nearly three thousand years ago, an ancient proverb that said precisely that was finally codified in writing:

> Train a child in the way that he should go,
> and when he is old he will not turn from it.[2]

Many people interpret this axiom as a promise—that if parents will raise ("train") their child with the "right" beliefs and values ("in the way that he *should* go," emphasis on "should"), the child will grow up to have good beliefs and values, and therefore good behavior. In short, the child will turn out "right."

However, this proverb is not a promise, but an observation—really a bit of seasoned wisdom about child-rearing. First of all, the Hebrew word translated "train" is better rendered as "dedicate." And the way the word is used means it is something essential, something parents must intentionally give themselves to. They can't be passive. They must dedicate themselves to "the way that the child should go."

What does that part of the proverb mean? In Hebrew, a person's "way" means their path in life—the journey they are on and how they walk that journey. In other words, how they live. In this proverb, the "way" involves the way of the child, "the way that *he* (the child) should go." Another way to translate it is "according to the dictates of his way," or, "according to what his way demands."

In short, the culture that devised this proverb recognized a core, universal reality about children—that each child has their own "bent," as we would say it today, some way of doing life to which they are inclined. Call it The Way of the Child. The Way of the Child is the same principle we are championing in this book: each child has their own giftedness.

This approach to childrearing has been around a long time, and we believe our world would benefit enormously if parents today returned to it.

## Through His Daughter's Eyes

Remember That Look, which we described in chapter 3? That Look silently sends the message "What's wrong with you?!" when the child does something different than the way the parent would do it. That Look is deeply hurtful, even damaging, to a child.

But there's an alternative to that approach. Instead of judgment, the parent could choose to respond with curiosity and wonder: "How interesting! I would never have thought to do that activity that way. I can see that this person (my child) is really different from me. What can I learn about them and perhaps the virtue of doing it their way through this unexpected behavior?"

On a recent Father's Day, Bill saw a Facebook post of a little girl, maybe five or six, beaming with delight as she stood beside her father's fancy car, holding the rock she had just used to scratch her Father's Day message into the side of the car: "B-E-S-T D-A-D-D-Y."

If ever there was a moment when That Look might be justified, that would be it, right? But let's do a thought experiment. Imagine if that little girl was fortunate enough to have a father who was radically dedicated to recognizing and responding to what The Way of the Child calls for?

Is it possible he might say, "Wow, princess, you've outdone yourself! I never expected a present like this for Father's Day. Tell me how you ever managed to come up with that idea."

Yes, yes, we know that most readers probably wonder what the father should say about the damage to the car's finish and the need to teach the child some responsibility and give her a lesson on not damaging someone else's property, etc. Clearly, that's how adults look at the situation.

But this father has dedicated himself to The Way of His Daughter. Over the five or six years of that girl's life, he has accustomed himself to looking at things *first* through her eyes, not his own. Why? Because he values the heart of his daughter infinitely more than what it will cost him to repair his BMW.

What's more, while he absolutely wants to help his daughter realize that her "gift" to him damaged his car and will prove quite costly, and of course he wants her to become a responsible person who respects others' property, he's learned something else over the five or six years of his daughter's life: every lesson must await its time. How much can a five-year-old understand about the cost of repairing a car? And at her age, how is she possibly going to understand that some grown-up word like "responsibility" somehow outweighs the pride she feels about her daddy and her desire to let the whole world know he's the greatest daddy ever by putting a message to that effect on the car that he drives everywhere?

There can't be many fathers who would do it, for sure, but let's say that father decides to drive his scratched car around town for a week before he takes it to the dealer for repair. Why? Because he is, in fact, the B-E-S-T D-A-D-D-Y. At least, he is to that little girl. And frankly, he's proud to be her daddy! And he doesn't mind when people at work and people at the store and people at stoplights do a double-take and laugh and even say, "Hey, buddy! I guess you're the best daddy, huh?" He just smiles and says, "Yeah, sometimes my daughter's creativity exceeds what I can afford!"

So what does he tell his daughter a couple of weeks later when she notices his repaired car and asks, "Daddy, what happened to my message on your car?"

"Well, princess, I took a bunch of pictures of it with my phone, and I've put those in my scrapbook about you so that I'll always be able to remember your message." (Later in the book we'll show a method for keeping a simple journal or scrapbook as a way of discovering your child's giftedness.) "That was a very special message. Thank you for letting me know you think I'm the best daddy. But you know what? I realized after driving around for a week that I was probably making all the other daddies who were seeing that message feel jealous. So I decided to have the car dealership paint over what you put there. We still have the pictures, and I'm so happy to be your daddy. But the fact that I'm the best daddy can just be a secret that we keep between us. What do you think, princess?"

## "You Still Have Your Giftedness"

Then he waits. He waits maybe eight or ten years until his daughter grows into her early teens. One night at dinner she launches into a story about a friend whose mom's car got keyed at the mall in an incident of "parking lot rage." An argument ensued after her mother pulled into a parking space just ahead of a guy who thought he should have gotten the space first. After an altercation, he took off in a rage and they went shopping. Then when they got back to their car, the side was all keyed and scratched with cuss words. "They think it was that guy."

Later after dinner, the father stops by his daughter's room. "Hey, princess, you got a minute? I want to show you something." Then he sits down and pulls out the scrapbook he's been keeping on his daughter's giftedness for fifteen or so years. He flips through, and then hands his daughter the pictures of his car with the message, B-E-S-T D-A-D-D-Y scratched into the side. "Do you remember this?"

The girl looks at the photos for a second, and then says, "Oh, wow! I had totally forgotten about this! But yeah, now I do remember. That was like Father's Day when I was like five or something, wasn't it?" She just stares at the pictures. And then suddenly she gets it. "Oh, my gosh!" she says with a laugh. "Oh, my gosh, I can't believe—Daddy, look what I did to your car!" And with that, tears start welling up in her eyes. "Oh, Daddy, I'm so sorry. I didn't mean to do that to your car. That must have cost you a fortune!"

"I know you're sorry, princess. It's okay. You were only five. You had no idea what kind of damage you were doing." After a pause he says, "I can't honestly say that I didn't care. I was *not* happy about the car! But your message meant so much more to me than the cost of a stupid paint job. Yeah, I have to admit, it would have been better if you'd used a crayon and a simple piece of construction paper." They both laughed. "But you were using your giftedness. And here we are, all these years later, having a good laugh over it. And I've probably been through three or four cars since then. But you still have your giftedness. And thanks to what you wrote back there and the pictures I took of it, I still have proof that I'm the best daddy."

Okay, maybe no parent like that really exists. But maybe they could. Because maybe it's not a damaged BMW. Maybe it's just a big pile of loamy soil in the backyard that you were going to use to sod your yard, and your kid has turned it into a mud bath. Maybe it's the mess all over the kitchen that your daughter has left from her effort to bake some muffins. Maybe it's the nerve-wracking bang of drums and clash of cymbals erupting from your adolescent son's room by the hour. Maybe it's your child's fixation with creatures in the wild, and they've brought yet another creepy, crawly, slimy, wiggly thing into your home.

Thanks to giftedness, children specialize in posing their parents with the same basic choice, again and again: "My child is perfectly happy, but their behavior seems (pick your term) mystifying, infuriating, frustrating, silly, reckless . . . " So how will you respond? With That Look? Or with curiosity and wonder? As the adult in this situation, whose interests will you favor?

Look, we're not saying that you always let your child "get their way." By no means! In addition to learning what their giftedness is, your child also must learn how to manage it responsibly. That often means setting limits and boundaries to its expression (more on that to come). As the parent, you have to help your child start learning (in age-appropriate ways) where those limits and boundaries are.

But setting limits and boundaries is to parenting what the sidelines are to soccer or football. Sure, they're part of the game in that they help define the field of play. But the game itself is about what happens on the field, between those sidelines. Likewise, parenting is all about paying attention to who your child is trying to be and what they are trying to do in light of their "way," their giftedness. Yes, sometimes you have to let them know they are out of bounds, or close to it. But beware of calling a foul just because their behavior is different from yours or creates a bit of inconvenience.

**Parenting is all about paying attention to who your child is trying to be.**

# the early years

# 6

# first look

We've already talked about how telling certain kinds of stories from one's life is key to discovering one's giftedness. But how does that work with a little one who doesn't have many (or any) words yet?

Infants and toddlers "tell" stories differently. Not about things that happened to them in the past. Rather, they tell their stories *in real time* by living out their giftedness right in front of you, using what we described earlier as *motivated behavior.*

That sets the stage for using a different model for discovering giftedness in children. It involves systematically or intentionally paying attention to and keeping track of their motivated behavior over time. Over a long time, actually—like five, ten, fifteen, or more years of your child's life. The aim is that by the time they get into their mid-teens, you end up with a treasure trove of clues pointing to their giftedness.

In this chapter we want to get you started on a method for how you can spot your child's motivated behavior and then record what you see for future reference (in chapter 18 we'll show you how those observations reveal a consistent pattern of giftedness).

To begin, let's consider what motivation is all about in the first place.

## What Motivates Us?

Did you know that motivation is a form of energy?[1] Whenever you do something, you exert a degree of energy to do it. For instance, when you go to work it takes energy, right? Buying groceries and getting them home requires energy. Doing your budget and bookkeeping demands a certain energy. Physical tasks like mowing the yard or working out at the gym definitely burn up some energy. And let's be honest, for some people, just getting out of bed in the morning takes up a lot of energy!

Where does that energy come from? Often it comes from outside of you through some form of external motivation.[2] At least, that's how it works for grown-ups. Fear, shame, manipulation—those are some negative motivators. More positive motivators would include money, yes, but also comfort, pleasure, and the powerful magnet of belonging. All of these examples of motivation, whether positive or negative, come from the outside—often in the service of The People in Charge.

**Internal motivation is to external motivation what fireworks are to a smoldering ember.**

Sometimes external motivation can seem rather powerful. Yet it's nothing compared the most powerful and effective means of motivating people. In reality, external motivation is incredibly weak. It only appears to be effective because people tend to respond to it with an initial burst of energy. But it has little power to sustain people's energy over time. People even find ways to avoid or defeat external motivators if they can. And as soon as those external drivers go away, people stop doing whatever it was they were supposedly "motivated" to do.

There is, however, another source of motivating energy, and we saw it during our visit to the playground in chapter 4. Remember how each child had selected the activity they wished to engage in, whether with other children or by themselves? Where did the energy come from to throw themselves with such abandon into their chosen pursuits? It came from within, from internal (or *intrinsic*) motivation.

Internal motivation is to external motivation what fireworks are to a smoldering ember. The latter you have to constantly blow air onto to keep it from dying out, whereas fireworks can't wait to explode in a burst of energy, beauty, and celebration.

Internal motivation is the most powerful force in the world when it comes to motivating human beings. That's because it comes from a place inside a person that says, "I *want* to do this," or, "I *get* to do this," or, "I *must* do this." Not, "I *have* to do this."

Infants and toddlers excel at trying to express intrinsic motivation because, unlike so many adults, they have not yet had the life squeezed out of them, leaving them susceptible to the many systems of external motivators described above. In other words, they don't know any better. They just show up in the world every day, trying to "be who they be."

Which is where you come in, as the parent. As your child encounters their world and tries to freely select what they will do or not do; what they will get interested in or disinterested in; what they will pay attention to or ignore altogether; what they will come back to or forget about; what they will delight in and what they will reject or even fear; whom they will seek out and whom they will bypass—as they manifest such behaviors (primitive though the behaviors may be), their first experience with The People in Charge is almost certainly going to be you, their parent.

What should you do?

## Everything Is Evidence

In the last chapter we looked at the story of Jaimie and her daughter, Danice. You'll recall that early on, Danice was a colicky baby. Like any good mother, Jaimie wanted to relieve her daughter's distress. And consistent with her own giftedness, she approached that task as a challenge to be surmounted.

There's nothing to fault Jaimie on in taking that approach. In the end, it proved quite effective. But can you see that she was looking at the situation through her own eyes? What if she had looked at it through the eyes of her daughter?

"How could she have possibly done that?" you might be asking. How can any parent know what is going on in the mind of a screaming newborn? Indeed, how do we even know that anything was going on in Danice's mind?

Well, we don't know, exactly. Except that if you buy our premise that a baby is an infant person, then you can more or less assume that something of the child's personhood is involved in *everything* about them—including colic.

Fast forward to five years later. As we've seen, Danice loves to sit at the playground and watch what's going on and make up rhymes in her head. We've also seen that at school a few years later, Danice is one of "the quiet ones" who sits back and watches what's going on—with the result that a teacher misidentifies her as "shy."

Question: Based on those two scenes alone—the playground and the schoolroom—what impression do we start to gain of Danice as a person? Well, apparently that she is someone who likely prefers to quietly absorb what is going on around her and fashion it into some sort of narrative, using words.

So what happens if that person we've just described is brought home *as a newborn* and suddenly immersed in surroundings that include the constant cacophony of a yappy Chihuahua (named Thanos), the intrusions of two smart phones, the blaring of a television, the glare of overhead lights, and the overstimulation of eager grandmothers, aunts, cousins, and others who insist on "holding the baby" and "comforting the baby" and showing "how good they are with babies"?

What happens is that Baby Danice—*being who she is*—feels overloaded. She can't yet talk. She can't yet walk away. She's pretty limited and primitive in how she can respond. So she does what babies can do: she cries. It's her only means of telling Mommy and everyone else that she'd much prefer to be able to sit back in peace and quiet and gently make sense of the world.

You may feel that we're speculating here. Except that Jaimie figured it out—albeit obliquely—by reasoning from her own experience with migraines.

Again, Jaimie did nothing wrong, and in fact did everything right to "fix" the situation. And no one can blame her for trying to fix it. Colic in a baby can kick the stuffing out of a parent! So much so that it can easily obliterate any awareness of what the child is actually doing.

But you see, there's more than just a baby with unrelenting colic. There's a *person* in Jaimie's arms. That means that in addition to trying to get to the bottom of the colic, Jaimie could have added one additional step. She could have pondered the question: Is Danice's colic telling me anything about who my baby is *as a person*? Jaimie also could have taken advantage of the rare, quiet windows when Danice was not screaming to perhaps get a glimpse of her personhood. Doing so would have itself been life-giving to Jaimie.

**You need to get in the habit of considering what your child's behaviors may be revealing about who they are.**

Babies get colic for many reasons, but the point is this: your child's personhood is involved in everything about him or her, so in a real sense, everything is evidence. As a parent, then, you need to get into the habit of considering what your child's behaviors may be revealing about who they are.

To help with that, let's put a finer point on what you should look for.

## Pay Attention to Your Child's Energy

By definition, whatever your child decides to do or focus on or move toward when *they* get to choose, the energy for that chosen behavior is coming from within. So that's what you want to pay attention to—their intrinsic, or self-motivated, energy.

And when we say, "you want to pay attention to," we of course mean you should include the observations of others who have been involved with your child and can lend perspective—relatives, trusted friends, neighbors, etc. Just make sure that you hold any and all observations lightly—no snap judgments—and always seek to frame them in positive language. Rather than say, "He doesn't quiet down easily" (which puts things negatively), say something like, "He seems to be especially sensitive to his surroundings and especially attuned to the person who is caring for him."

With that said, here are some specifics to watch for:

### *What does your child focus on? What holds their attention?*

Motivated behavior always involves concentration (although not every instance of concentration stems from motivated behavior). You know how that works yourself if you've ever gotten "into" a project or activity so much that you lost track of the time.

Your child does the same thing—again, in primitive ways at first, but with growing sophistication over time. For one child it may be shapes. For another colors. For another sounds. For another how things "work." Given the endless possibilities available in your child's strange new world, they could end up focusing on almost anything: the dog's fur, a water faucet, a particular toy, a certain food, what happens when they look in a mirror, the buttons on an Xbox, a potted plant.

It doesn't really matter what the object of their focus turns out to be. What matters—what you should take note of—is that something is holding your child's attention. Or, to look at the situation through their eyes: they are letting go of other possibilities in order to concentrate on something of their own choosing. That suggests motivated behavior. You don't need to ask *why* they are choosing that thing. Just notice that they've chosen it.

One little boy fixated on how he could drop a spongey ball. From high. From low. From his hand. From a table. From his high chair. From his bed. From his playpen. On the floor. On his foot. On his head. On his nose. As long as he could drop that ball, he was a happy camper!

Another two-year-old developed a fascination with the new dishwasher that her parents had installed in the kitchen. She would come and sit by the appliance for extended periods of time. She even made it her "friend," talking to it, smiling at it, showing it to her stuffed animals, singing songs to it.

You may never know what those activities "mean," and if they do mean something (i.e., if they fit into a long-term pattern of giftedness), you can't and won't know it until many years later (more on that to come). But again, don't worry about interpreting the behavior right now. Just notice it. Notice that your child is focusing on something.

### What activities does your child come back to again and again?

This follows from what we've just said. It's one thing for your child to focus on some random activity for a while, but then never pay much attention to it again. But what if they keep coming back to the same activity over and over? That repeated engagement is a telltale sign that the activity is stimulating something related to their giftedness.

You can use that observation to further engage them. For example, if your child seems to love books, you should offer them more books. And if they push the book away or squirm or turn away, then think back to something you've seen them glom onto before and create a space for that activity.

However, don't feel like you have to orchestrate your child's every waking minute. It's actually helpful to leave baby on her own for a few unfilled moments so she can do whatever she chooses to do without external direction of any kind. Likewise, allow your child lots of freedom to change preferences. One child will move from thing to thing while another will attend to just one thing for a while. Either way is fine because this is not about you showing them what to do, but about them showing you who they are. As they are growing and developing, they are expressing lots of natural ability, even if it's still in primitive forms.

### What does your child get excited about?

Internal motivation is naturally enthusiastic. It eagerly seeks expression. So what is your child eager to do? Not so much from a "consumption" standpoint, like eat chocolate ice cream, or have you push them in the swing at the playground, or let them crawl into bed with you during a thunderstorm. But what activities demand something from them that they are only too eager to do?

When we were small children, our parents occasionally arranged for us to spend the day with one of their friends who lived nearby. Among the activities the mother had us do was one we had never encountered before: mixing up plaster of Paris, pouring it into rubber molds, letting it dry while we did other things, then removing the figurines from the molds and painting them in time to dry before our mom picked us up to go home.

We both *loved* making plaster of Paris models! Bev remembers that this fun mom seemed as excited as we were to do that activity with us. She allowed us to make a mess and had everything we needed there to make the activity fun for us. She also enjoyed the fact that we were getting to play in a new place with new kids, doing something we had never done before that everyone could enjoy, and then have something to take home at the end. Bill remembers how cool the figurines looked after they had been painted, and how he could display them in his room at home.

What kinds of things is your child *eager* to do? Helping measure out ingredients for making cookies? Turning the pages of a songbook while you play the piano? Raking leaves? Feeding the hamster? Putting the crayons back in the box in just the right order? Going with you to get the mail out of the mailbox? Make the sounds of all the animals in a storybook? Making a list of what they want to do each day? Driving by the statue of a fawn at a nearby greenspace?

To be sure, not every day offers space and time for indulging your child's "love to do" activities. But staying mindful of activities that cause them to come alive and creating opportunities to do those things opens up a treasure trove of possibilities for observing them at their best.

Again, it doesn't really matter *what* they are eager to do. It's their energy, their enthusiasm, their excitement that you want to pay attention to. The activity itself may seem mundane—at least, to you, especially as an adult. But to your child, there's something bordering on magic taking place inside. Something about the activity fills them with exuberance—something they probably can't even identify quite yet, and therefore something you have no way to begin to know about yet.

### What suddenly "wakes up" or energizes your child?

This is an extension of what we've just said. The idea here is that your child is just going along, taking life as it comes. Then suddenly something happens! Something enters the picture and they are instantly full of life and energy and excitement. The change is unmistakable—and totally unexpected. In the blink of an eye they may switch from total boredom or lethargy or fussiness to intense focus and total engagement.

Whatever you do, pay attention! You can't really know at that moment exactly what is going on, but something has just intersected with your child's giftedness. If they're old enough, draw them out a little bit to find out more: "Oh, you like that? Is that fun? What's fun? Tell Daddy." Younger children usually can't tell you with words what makes them come alive, but noticing how they go about an activity and/or engaging with them as they do it often leads to great insight.

We know a five-year-old who loves to put things *into* something else. That's a pretty simple activity, but one she takes great delight in. She loves to put the flowers she's found on a walk into a vase. She loves to line up her princess figurines in their fairyland castle. She loves to put the cracked eggs into the bowl of batter. We don't know what putting things into something else means for her yet, but we don't need to. We just need to pay attention to the fact that she gains energy from that activity.

Not long ago, Bev spent the day with this little one. As a present, Bev gave her a summer outfit that Bev had bought for Molly, the girl's special doll. The outfit included a tiny purse. The girl was delighted with the clothes, but the first thing she latched onto was the purse. She eagerly asked Bev to help her find something to put into Molly's purse. There were some sunglasses that came with the outfit, but they were too big for the purse (who in the world designed that?). So the girl began searching all around the room, testing one thing after another until she pulled open a drawer and discovered an old coin in a box. "Something Molly would love!" she exclaimed.

"Do you think Molly is going to spend it or save it?" Bev asked her.

"Oh, she wants to save it!" the little girl declared with a smile, and into the purse it went.

### What consistently makes your child smile or giggle or show some other positive response?

Motivated behavior involves satisfaction and delight, so it makes sense that your child will have positive emotional reactions to things that prove satisfying and meaningful (to them). As always, the possibilities for the source of their joy are endless: The way light refracts off a cloud. The feel of a cat's tail slipping through their hand. The taste of a peanut butter cookie. The sound of a car's horn. The sight of ducklings following in a line behind their mother. The way water splashes from a puddle that they jump into.

**Is "hurry" the story of your life?**

Busy parents usually take their children's smiles and laughter for granted—and sometimes even resent the fact that they are "wasting time" when "we're in a hurry" to go somewhere.

Let's say a word about hurry: Is that the story of your life? You're always going somewhere, getting somewhere, late to being somewhere. As if the most important things in life are always in the *next* moment rather than the present one.

Think about that! Here's your small child, pausing to respond to something that has filled their soul with delight because their soul was made to delight in that something. Everything in them is saying, "Wow! Look at this. Do you see? This is wonderful! This is amazing! This makes me so happy!" Everything in them and all the emotion coming out of them is also saying, "Look at me! Look at what matters to me!" It's a golden moment.

Meanwhile, you're are on a different clock. And because you're the parent, you're The Person in Charge. So of course, it's your clock and priorities and what matters to you that are going to prevail. A child is standing in the way of that. So next thing you know, the child is hearing, "Stop wasting time! Hurry up! We're late! Get in the car!"

And a golden moment slips away.

Here's a suggestion: the next time you're in a rush to get your child off to daycare so you can get to your meeting—and on the way to the car your child squats down to smile at a roly-poly crawling across the walkway—instead of yanking them by the arm to get them in the car, walk back and just stand by them for a moment, silently saying to yourself, *This, too, matters, because my child matters. I choose to see my child in this moment of wonder.*

And after pausing for the sake of your child, you might say, "What a wonderful thing that you noticed the roly-poly. Let's come back and look at her some more later. For now, we need to get you to daycare." And having celebrated the moment and your child in that way, the two of you move on. Then when you show up at your meeting ninety seconds late, you can say, "Sorry to be a couple minutes late, but my child had something really important to show me as we were walking out the door." (Hint: what your child had to show you was not a roly-poly, but a glimpse into their giftedness.)

### What does your child keep asking for?

Since giftedness is a *pattern* of behavior, it makes sense to pay attention to what your child keeps coming back to, especially by way of requests.

Day after day, two-and-a-half-year-old Jillian asks her mother whether she can go outside. It doesn't matter whether it's sunny, cloudy, raining, snowing—Jillian wants to go outside.

It's a simple enough request. But for Jillian's mother, it becomes a bit of a bother because it places an imposition on the mother. She can't just let Jillian go outside by herself, so if the mother agrees to the request, she has to go outside with her daughter. That means dropping whatever she happened to be doing inside at that moment.

Nor does there seem to be rhyme or reason as to why Jillian wants to go outside. Sometimes she plays on the swing set. Sometimes she goes and looks in the flowerbed. Sometimes she sits down on the lawn and sings to herself. Sometimes she wants Mommy to watch her run around. Sometimes she chases the cat. Sometimes she just looks up in the sky. To an adult like Jillian's mother, who has a lot of responsibility at her job—and so she almost always has brought work home to do—going outside so her daughter can do whatever it is she wants to do out there seems like a colossal waste of time.

But as with the roly-poly child above, a parent's agenda can so easily blow past the golden moments when a child is revealing something about who they are.

If Jillian's mother were to pay attention, she would notice the most important thing, which happens to be hidden in plain sight: Jillian keeps asking to go outside. That's all—but that's it! Apparently she loves to go outside. Again, given Jillian's age, it's impossible to know what to make of that. But our recommendation to Jillian's mother would be to just go with it as much as possible.

"Going with it" means that Jillian's mother just accepts that for the next couple of years she's going to frequently need to be outside with Jillian until the girl is old enough be outside by herself. So Mom plans for what she can do with her own time whenever she's outside with Jillian.

This is part of what it means to be the parent of a toddler. There are so many things that a toddler can't do. Yet their giftedness is surging to express itself. So they often try to enlist the help of a parent (or other family member) in order to do whatever that thing is that gives them such satisfaction. They may also express their giftedness in a not-so-positive way—especially if they are frustrated due to not having grown sufficient wings yet to do it like they want to.

We must point out that there's an invaluable hidden benefit to noticing and, as much as possible, "going with" whatever your child keeps asking for. In a subtle but powerful way you are communicating, "I see you. I notice you. You matter. What's more, I'm *for* you. I'm behind you all the way! I can see that you love to be outdoors (or ride your bike while I watch, or have me read that same book to you yet again, or let you mix the cake batter, or play pick-up sticks, or whatever your child's repeated request happens to be). I can see you love that, so I want to make it possible for you to do what you love, to do what fills you with life and energy and joy." In short, "going with" the repeated request is a way of showing your child you love them.

### Keeping a Giftedness Journal

As you practice all of these habits for noticing your child's motivated behavior, remember to keep your eye on the long game. Remember, this is part of a simple but powerful methodology aimed at discovering things about your child's giftedness so that you can parent them in a way that fits who they are—according to Your Child's Way.

That discovery process happens *over years*. So you need a means of collecting your observations about your child's motivated behavior (along with questions, notes, reminders), so as not to forget them. To do that, we strongly recommend you keep a journal where you record simple descriptions about the kinds of activities and behaviors we've described above:[3]

- What your child has focused on and paid attention to
- What your child keeps coming back to
- What your child has gotten excited about
- What your child has suddenly gotten energized by
- What your child has shown some sort of positive emotional response to
- What your child keeps asking for
- What things your child chooses to play with

You can call this journal Erin's Giftedness Journal, or Thomas's Special Stories, or Observations About Zachery, or My Memories of Maleka, or whatever else you'd like to call it. The point is that you have a designated place to collect your observations of your child that seem noteworthy in terms of motivation and behavior.

To make this part of the exercise work, you have to be reasonably intentional about writing entries into the journal, because this is something you'll need to do over many years during your child's childhood and teen years. But having said that, whatever you do, don't feel like you have to make this a fancy, time-consuming project! We're talking very, very simple, brief, one- or two-sentence entries, maybe twice a week, if that. (If you're inclined to write more, go for it!)

Here are some examples of what we mean by giftedness journal entries:

- Today Baby Enzo seemed transfixed watching a lava lamp that Michael (his father) put on the table near his crib.

- When Grandma and her three friends stopped by this afternoon to see Abby, Abby lit up with the biggest smile and reached right out to them. I thought she was going to jump out of my arms, she was so excited! She was making all kinds of noises like she was happy.

- Ian had been fussy all afternoon. But as soon as we got home, Tricia (his older sister) put him on the sofa while I unloaded the car. She was singing to him, and he sat happily listening to her for at least twenty minutes without a peep. I've never seen him do that before.

- Once again, Hattie begged me to take her to the zoo today. I don't know, it's something about the otters. I swear, she could sit and watch the otters for hours!

- I'm completely mystified! I've tried for weeks—really months—to get Liam to eat green vegetables like broccoli or peas. He simply wouldn't do it. Then after Ben got home on leave yesterday, I cooked up his favorite meal of steak, potatoes, and peas. I couldn't believe it when Ben scooped up a spoonful of peas and dropped them right into Liam's mouth without the slightest pushback. Why was Liam willing to eat peas for him but not me? Go figure!

What you're doing in this activity is collecting data. Remember earlier when we said that everything is evidence? Keeping a giftedness journal means you're building an ongoing database of evidence about your child's motivated behavior as they get older. When we get to chapter 18, we'll show you how to evaluate that evidence to see consistent patterns of giftedness.

Again, we ask you *not* to look for patterns yet. That's the biggest temptation that parents experience once they grasp the methodology of our approach. The process is simple enough: make some observations, then look for some patterns. Armed with that formula, parents often want to jump to conclusions. But that's almost always a mistake.

It's a mistake, first, because there's rarely a one-to-one, straight-line correspondence between the primitive behavior of a child and the later, fuller expression of their personhood as an adult. One little boy loves to watch the garbage truck come by and the sanitation workers pick up the trash. "That's what I want to do when I grow up!" he declares with all the certainty of a four-year-old. His parents are crestfallen. But they need not be. How is the boy to know that his delight in solving practical problems in the outdoors that benefit people (which sanitation work does) will someday lead to a thoroughly fulfilling and productive career in civil engineering?

Or say your child takes a keen interest in knives and sharp objects. That means they're going to grow up to pursue a life of crime, right? Probably not.

Childhood is the time to collect the data, not to interpret it. You can't yet draw definitive conclusions because it's only limited data. But later on (meaning years later on), as the data mounts up, a bigger picture will begin to take shape.

If you lock down on an interpretation too early, you're liable to typecast your child and assign them a label. And it may well be a label that fails to honor the true nature of the gift: "shy" (as we saw with Danice), "little troublemaker," "the bug kid," "our professor," "Little Miss Know-It-All," etc. Or it might be a label that you intend as positive and filled with high expecta-

**A disability never negates giftedness.**

tions, but it's still only an exaggerated (and potentially misleading) caricature of your child: "Our superstar," "The Queen," "the enforcer," "Johnny Rock Star," "Wheeler Dealer."

## A Word About Disabilities

In helping parents begin to recognize the giftedness of their children, we're occasionally confronted with the parent of a disabled child who says to us, in effect, "This talk about giftedness is all well and good. But you don't understand. My child has a disability, so that changes everything."

Our response: actually not. A disability never negates giftedness. While the realities of contending with a disability cannot be overlooked and should not be minimized, the fact remains that *the child is not their disability; the child is a person.* Which means that the child with a disability has their own unique giftedness every bit as much as does the child with no apparent disability.

No one knows that better than Bill's friend, Tom Landis, a restaurateur and founder of Howdy Homemade Ice Cream. Tom and his friend, Manuel Ramirez—the first person he ever hired—worked with numerous special needs organizations to learn how to hire, train, and employ people with Down syndrome and autism. Howdy Homemade is entirely managed and staffed by people with special needs because

Tom's mission in life is to change the way businesses employ people with special needs. At Howdy, every team member has a vital role to play, and every one of them is positioned where their giftedness can be expressed most effectively.[3]

Again, we would never want to minimize the challenges of parenting a child with a disability. But it's a mistake to focus primarily on your child's disability and see them primarily through that lens. Because that's not their identity. Their personhood is not their autism, their Down syndrome, their dyslexia, their impairment in hearing or seeing, their spina bifida. Those are limitations. Those are challenges, for sure.

But regardless of the disability, your child is a person who is seeking to engage the world in their own signature way. *That* person should be the focus of your relationship.

# 7

# preschool: the golden years

The legendary Fred Rogers made a brilliant career on PBS out of the simple observation that preschool children tend to take things literally. So much so that after three seasons of "Mister Rogers' Neighborhood," he changed the lyrics to his signature song, "Tomorrow," which ended each episode. Beginning in Season 4, Rogers sang the original lyric on Mondays through Thursdays: "I'll be back, when the day is new." But on Fridays, he changed his promise to: "I'll be back, when the week is new."[1] He didn't want any child wondering why the show wasn't being aired on Saturday.

Young children indeed take things literally. But in many ways the same could be said for the children themselves: they also want to be taken literally. Meaning that they want to be accepted at face value, for who they are. They've not yet learned to edit their behavior in order to make it acceptable to others. They just show up and "be who they be."

That's why the preschool years are in many ways the Golden Years in terms of revealing your child's giftedness. You get to observe it in its raw, unvarnished state, before they have heard all the voices telling them how they are "supposed" to behave. Indeed, at The Giftedness Center, when we listen to people tell us their stories from throughout their life, they often recall scenes from their preschool years that many times turn out to be emblematic of the way they have most naturally been approaching life ever since.

## It's Not Just Play

But many parents miss those Golden Years because they don't take their child's behavior seriously. To them, the child is "just playing" most of the time. Why should anyone pay attention to that?

Once again, we appeal to the wisdom of Fred Rogers: "Play is often talked about as if it were a relief from serious learning. But for children, play is serious learning. Play is the real work of childhood."[2]

That's a profound insight. Here's your preschooler—now diaperless, mobile, coordinated, talkative, interactive, inquisitive. Suddenly the world is posing options that were never available before. What will your child do? What will they choose to do? What would they like to do? How will they choose to do it? Whatever it is, your child goes to work on it with all the serious abandon of "play."

That's your golden opportunity as a parent. As they play, take note of where their energy goes and what behaviors they consistently choose. Let them take the lead in what they want to play with and how, and be willing to participate if they bring you in. Then later, record your observations of their behavior in their giftedness journal, as described in the previous chapter.

Here are a few of the many categories you should pay attention to:

- *Toys.* What toys does your child keep going back to? How do they play with those toys (children often use toys for other purposes than the toy was designed for)? Is a toy just a thing, or is there some special way in which the toy itself holds the child's interest and attention? What happens if, for some reason, your child cannot find a favorite toy? Over time, does your child lose interest in a toy and move on to other toys, or does a toy lead to "higher level" toys (e.g., a tricycle is replaced by a bicycle, or crayons give way to watercolors, or Potato Head leads to the Potato Head Family)?

We think it's a good idea to offer your child a wide range of toys, if possible, especially ones that fire up their imagination or that invite them to stretch their skills, efforts, or wits. Too many toys nowadays merely entertain, turning children into spectators. You want your child to be an actor, to be involved and engaged in actually playing. That's where the giftedness gets activated—when your child is doing an activity, even if that activity is going on inside their head.

- *Games.* Are there particular games that your child asks to play (whether board games or physical activities)? What aspect of the game seems to hold your child's attention? What part of the game seems to elicit the most delight? How does your child react when the game doesn't go their way? How does your child respond to winning the game? To losing? Has your child developed any tricks or strategies to increase their effectiveness at playing the game? Do they seem to enjoy being challenged by difficult puzzles or games that are hard to win?

- *Friends.* Who are the children your child prefers to play with? What activities do they do together? Who initiates those activities? When your child is playing with someone else, what do you see your child doing and what do you see the other child doing? Are there ways in which your child acts differently when playing with others than by themselves? Do they just have one or two close friends, or do they always prefer to be surrounded by a group of friends?

- *Problem Solving.* What happens when your child is presented with a "problem," meaning something they haven't yet learned and so they must figure it out—e.g., opening a new tube of toothpaste, retrieving something that has fallen behind the bed, getting a cup from the kitchen cabinet, tying their shoes, cleaning up some spilled milk, etc.? Perhaps they jump right in and start trying different strategies. Perhaps they pause for a moment to take stock of the situation. Perhaps they try and enlist someone to help them. Perhaps they just give up. They might start calling for you to do something. Or they might imitate what they've seen you do. There are countless possibilities. But whatever their response, it likely offers clues as to the seeds of their giftedness.

- *Living Things.* Your child's interactions with the various creatures they encounter take things to a whole new level in terms of making observations about their giftedness. We heartily encourage you to take your child to a zoo, aquarium, farm, ranch, or some other setting dominated by animals. While those kinds of venues tend to be controlled, it's fun to watch how a child reacts to the different species they see.

    Pay attention to the comments they make and the questions they ask, and join them in their learning. What do they focus on? What do they find interesting about the animals? Do they talk about "what I would do if I were in charge of the animals"? What do they most remember about them later on? Do they take an interest in any particular animal? If so, follow the trail of that interest and affirm it by opening doors for further discovery (e.g., online resources, books at the library, videos).

    Pets bring interactions with the animal kingdom right into your home. Unlike an animal at the zoo, a pet personalizes the relationship between your child and an animal. Indeed, many pets essentially become members of the family over time—which in itself can offer some interesting glimpses into your child's giftedness.

When Bill's three daughters were young, their mother learned that rats make great pets. So over several years, a succession of beloved rats lived with the Hendrickses: Honey, Honeybar, Napoleon (remembered as the greatest of all the rats), Silver, Grayling (who had three babies: Sprite, Slice, and 7-Up), Coco, Hershey (who learned to run a maze), two near the end named Piña Colada and Strawberry Daiquiri (not sure where those names came from), and Alex (go figure), to name a few. From the names alone, you can probably guess that the rats proved to be a huge stimulation to the giftedness of Bill's daughters!

Rats may not be to your liking (they surely were not to Aunt Bev's liking; she would only visit when those critters were safely locked in their cages!). But is there some other species your family is drawn to? If so, pay attention to the relationship between that pet and your child. Do they try and make it a playmate? Do they view it as a creature to be cared for? To be instructed or trained? To be shown off and bragged about? Does the pet reveal anything about your child's sense of responsibility? Does the pet inspire your child to make up stories or draw pictures of it?

Meanwhile, there are also the living things that your child comes across spontaneously: the earthworm, the spider, the caterpillar, the garden snake, numerous varieties of birds, squirrels, mice and rats, perhaps opossums and raccoons, deer, frogs, fish. As a parent, you do well to get into the habit of paying attention and responding to what your child notices about these creatures.

Naturally, you also have to be concerned about your child's safety as they encounter creatures in the wild. But as you do so, consider that your reaction will tend to heavily influence your child's initial perceptions about a species.

For example, suppose you and your three-year-old are weeding the garden together, and as you push a plant to the side you suddenly see the grey and yellow lines of a tiny garter snake that is slithering to get out of the way. If you let out a bloodcurdling shriek, grab your child in your arms, and make a beeline for the house, you've just eliminated any possibility of allowing your child to spontaneously and naturally have their own experience of the creature.

Perhaps a better alternative would be to first quietly master your own fright. Then take a deep breath, gently grasp your child's hand, and say something like, "Oh, Joanna, look here! It's a little garter snake. See it?" Then let your child react however they react. They may display fear (again, a lot depends on what they've seen others do previously in similar circumstances). But they might just as easily display curiosity. Or wonder. Or surprise. Of course, they might also show disinterest. Anything is possible. But nothing is really "wrong."

- *Interests*. From her earliest days, Bev was always interested in stories. Stories someone told. Stories someone read. Stories someone acted out. Many a Saturday when she was a child, she curled up on her bed after breakfast, buried her nose in a book, and stayed that way until she had finished the very last word of the story. What's more, she would read the book again and again throughout the course of her childhood.

  Children tend to gravitate toward certain favorite activities and interests. In other words, they show more energy for those pursuits than others. Sometimes they will come back to a certain activity as often as they can, and the pursuit of that interest may last over years, if not indefinitely.

  Having said that, it's also worth noting that other children possess a curiosity that predisposes them to engage a wide range of interests rather than stick with any one thing. So a parent has to be careful not to freeze-frame their child into some particular interest.

But it's worth asking: what are your child's compelling interests? For one little boy it was the fish in the creek near his house. Once he discovered them, he spent almost every hour of his free time observing those fish, learning how to catch them, reading up on their habits, and developing something of an expertise in the fish of his area. That interest lasted all the way through high school. Indeed, as a grown man with a family of his own, he still delights in going fishing.

For another child it may be a vegetable garden. For another it could be geography and a fascination with different places in the world. Some children cultivate an in-depth knowledge of certain sports and their players. For others it is the imaginary worlds of superheroes. Still others are drawn toward history, or rocks, or the stars, or drawing, or making music, or acting out a role.

**There's a high correlation between childhood interests and what people end up doing with their lives as adults.**

What if your child doesn't seem particularly interested in any one thing? That's fine. But don't shy away from taking the initiative to introduce them to something they've never overtly expressed interest in. Sometimes by taking the first step to start a garden with them or involve them in baking cookies or get them singing with you, you may awaken their giftedness.

You might be interested to know that there's a high correlation between childhood interests and what people end up doing with their lives as adults. Raw giftedness plus time and opportunity can lead a person to some amazing accomplishments.

For example, John James Audubon, the legendary nineteenth-century naturalist, spent his childhood out in the woods, observing birds. Mega-billionaire investor Warren Buffett grew up in Omaha doing just about any activity having to do with numbers. And Southwest Airlines pilot Tammie Jo Shults, who calmly landed SWA #1380 after an engine exploded and shrapnel tore a hole in the aircraft's fuselage, grew up on a ranch in New Mexico, where day after day she watched military jets from a nearby base practicing their maneuvers. That childhood fascination with flight inspired her to dream of—and act on—becoming a pilot.[3]

But as we say, don't fret if you can't identify some overarching activity or subject that your child has latched onto. There's nothing wrong with them. It may be that they are not yet old enough for something to have captivated their attention. Just let them develop at their own pace. But do keep an eye out for what happens.

And for many kids, it's not the interest or the activity that matters so much as the people participating with them in the interest or activity. It's not about the *what* they are doing as much as the *who* they are doing it with.

• *Questions.* A growing body of research suggests that language development probably begins before a child is even born, as they pick up sounds and other language cues in the womb. Then when they enter the world, the learning curve rises like a hockey stick, and a child is typically capable of real, back-and-forth, turn-taking dialogue by age 3. But from there the child starts to acquire a profoundly powerful linguistic tool: the ability to ask questions. That's like arming them with the algorithm to Google! It means no adult is off-limits, nor is any subject.

You, the parent, will be most in the line of fire. Not all

preschoolers are question-factories, but many are. Especially the question, *Why?* "Mommy, why are there clouds?" "Daddy, why do dogs bark?" "Why are trees green?" "Why do I yawn?" "Why is it dark at night?" "Why do you always call Mommy/Daddy 'honey'?" "Why can't we fly like birds do?" "Why did my friend's daddy have to go away?" "Why are you crying?" "Why do you and Mommy/Daddy sleep by yourselves?" "Why did Grandma die?" "Why do I have to brush my teeth?" And of course, the ultimate of them all: "But *why?*"

A short time later, the *When?* and *How?* questions also start coming: "When will my baby sister come?" "When will it be time to go on our vacation?" "When is Grandpa going to take me fishing again?" "How do the lights know when to come on?" "How does the grass grow?" "How does your phone work?" "How are babies made?"

It's interesting that a great deal has been written to help parents find ways to shut down this endless stream of questions. That kind of makes sense from the standpoint of parents. After all, it's easy to feel worn out after your preschooler has asked you close to a hundred questions over the course of a day.

But in turn, it's also interesting that none of that advice seems to suggest two obvious, honest answers to yet the hundred-and-first question your child asks you: (1) "Wow, that's a great question you're asking. I'll tell you what, ask me that again tomorrow. I'm just so tired right now that I don't think I have the energy to answer any more questions today"; or (2) "I don't know. Let's you and me find someone who might be able to answer that question. What do you say?"

Most of the time your child's questions are not an attempt to see how smart you are, but rather just a normal part of their curiosity about the world. However, if you look for patterns among their questions, you may also detect some subtle but consistent themes underlying their interrogations.

For example, some children are bent on finding out how things work. Some want to understand how things are connected. Others seem to want to know which forces, factors, and figures affect the rest. Others seem fascinated by learning new information that tops whatever they've heard before, and the wonder of greater discovery. Still others are interested in finding out things that will arm them with new competence, power, or control over their world.

- *Imagination.* We've pointed out that giftedness is often best expressed when your child gets to *choose* the activity. Well, nowhere does a child have more freedom to choose than in what they dream about in their imagination. Imagination is like the ultimate Etch A Sketch.[4] Not only can one create whatever they want, they have total control over what they come up with. If they don't like the outcome, or they're tired of the concept, or they decide to create something else—no problem! They can just shake their head (just as one shakes an Etch A Sketch to "blank out" the screen) and begin anew.

So what imaginative creations does your child come up with? Do they spin little stories with characters who interact? Do they describe *what would happen if* _____? Do they picture themselves in a certain place, or portraying a certain role, or able to do a certain thing? Do they like to play dress-up with the family dog (or their little brother) and act out a scenario? Do they tell you about a secret place that only they know about? Do they take a discarded box and turn it into their own make-believe world?

Not only is the nature of your child's imaginative play worth noting, but also whether they return to some of the same themes or scripts again and again. Do they always end up in the role of a teacher, instructing their stuffed animals day after day? Do they keep setting up seemingly insurmountable challenges again and again, always vanquishing them using superhero-like powers? Do their fantasies often involve the rescue of this, that, or the other, where time and again they end up saving the day? Are they always on a quest to find something that has gone missing: the lost shoe, the lost LEGO block, the lost ribbon, the lost bar of soap?

Remember, imagination allows your child to do things they are not yet able to do (but wish they could) and go places they are not yet able to go (but wish they could). In other words, their imagination gives them agency—ability—before their time. What better way to observe what and where your child dreams of doing and going, deep down in their young heart, than to observe their imagination at work!

# 8

## shaping the clay

n the last two chapters we've given you a strategy for making and recording observations about your child's motivated behavior as a means of beginning to discover their giftedness. It really boils down to simply paying attention and making a habit of jotting down what you see. That can easily take place within the ordinary, everyday experiences of your family.

### Passive Parenting

Ironically, though, ordinariness is exactly why so many parents overlook the countless clues to giftedness that their child is constantly offering them. Motivated behavior is usually commonplace. The child is "just" playing. We are "only" going to the store. It's "just" a silly game.

In other words, the significance of the moment is lost in plain sight. Giftedness can be expressing itself right before a parent's eyes, but it gets overlooked because the behavior is normal.

For that reason, we challenge you: stay alert to your child's normal! We're not asking you to start second-guessing every moment of your child's day. But we are encouraging you to *pay attention*. Don't be a passive parent when it comes to your child's giftedness. Paying attention is actually a pretty easy task because the giftedness is there, and it's always seeking to express itself. You don't have to do anything to make it happen. Just watch what happens, and record what you see in your child's giftedness journal.

As we say, that's pretty easy. But unfortunately, being a passive parent is even easier. In fact, it's never been so easy, thanks to all our devices and screens and TV programs intentionally designed to capture and hold both our child's attention and our own. Those endless streams of content fill the spaces of endless possibilities with someone else's agenda.

Or, to put it another way: you know that video you bought for your preschooler—the one with the charming story brought to life in a way that is tailor-made for a child their age? Well, it's hijacking their mind. Oh, there's nothing inherently wrong with a video. But used indiscriminately, that engaging input begins to crowd out the ideas that could have been generated from your child's own imagination. Especially when one video becomes one after another, as is happening for a whole generation of children today.

What's more, whenever Junior is happily engrossed with a screen, he's not engaged socially with anyone else. That's bad enough for Junior, but it can end up bad for Junior's parents as well because it allows parenting to recede into the background. It's a common sight nowadays to see families where one parent is talking nonstop on their phone, the other is flipping through social media, and their children are riveted to their own devices. Everyone's together while each is off in their own little world. We can't help but mourn for all the missed, fleeting moments—moments when those parents could have been present to the wonder of the children.

## Proactive Parenting

So what if you decide you're not going to be that passive parent but rather a *proactive* parent who excels at this parenting thing? Well, then, here's what you can do: expose your preschooler to lots of different experiences that will offer them a variety of stimuli to respond to. We're talking about trips to the zoo or arboretum; singing, music, and musical instruments; shopping trips and errands; vacations or even just simple day trips; interactions with animals (dog-sitting, the adopt-a-pet kiosk at the shopping mall, a video on animals in the wild, etc.); games (board games, activity games, preschool-level sports); pretend and make-believe; craft projects; "help" in the kitchen; counting or naming exercises; "camping out" in the backyard; taking walks; and of course lots of telling stories and reading to your child. In truth, almost any activity that you and your family would be involved in can be made into a fruitful moment in which to observe your child's giftedness.

But you can't just be passive!

## "I'm Going to Be a Jockey!"

More than anything else, Isabella wants her son, Antonio, to grow up to be a strong, confident man with a sense of purpose and direction in life. So she is "all in" on this idea of trying to discover clues as to her son's giftedness.

One Saturday morning in the spring, five-year-old Antonio runs into the kitchen to tell his mother something about horses. She can't figure out what he's talking about. But later when she turns on the TV, she learns that this is Kentucky Derby Day.

Sure enough, when the broadcast finally begins that afternoon, Antonio has a front row seat in front of the television. For the next hour and a half he sits transfixed, taking in every detail about the horses, the jockeys, the trainers, the singing of "My Old Kentucky Home," the Call to the Post, Riders Up!, the stately parade to the starting gates, the loading of each horse into its gate, the bell and explosion of the horses out of the chute, the turn, the stretch, the far turn, the home stretch, the roaring of the crowd, the finish line, the winners screaming and hugging, the endless interviews, the roses adorning the winner. It all seems magical to him.

And he can't stop talking about it at dinner after the race. Finally he declares, "When I grow up, I'm going to be a jockey!"

The next morning, Isabella finds Antonio on the couch, riding one of the cushions as if he is astride a horse. He pays her no attention. He is lost in his imagination, talking excitedly to himself as he mimics the rocking rhythm of the jockeys he watched on the previous afternoon.

Isabella has never seen her son so taken with an activity. She feels sure he is telling her something about his giftedness (indeed he is!). He sounded so determined and insistent in his vow to become a jockey. The idea seems far-fetched to Isabella. But who knows? Maybe she should at least let him explore his newfound interest.

So the next day, after dropping her son at day care and going to work, Isabella goes online to look for horseback riding lessons in their area. She finds a stable that specializes in teaching children. But it would be pretty expensive for her as a single parent.

The cost causes her to stop and hesitate. For the rest of the day she mulls it over. Then that evening after dinner, she once again finds Antonio riding his imaginary horse on the couch. That pushes her over the edge. The next morning Isabella calls the stable and arranges a lesson for the next Saturday.

The day comes, and Isabella drives Antonio out to the stable. It's a well-kept place, and the personnel are very friendly. When the lesson begins, an instructor takes the six children in the class inside the barn, and Isabella sits at a picnic table reviewing her email.

An hour later, Antonio exits the barn, and they climb into their car. Isabella can't wait to hear about the lesson. But to her surprise, Antonio describes it as merely "okay." She presses into that to find out more and hears that being around the horses was "fun." That sounds like moving in the right direction. But she is not seeing anywhere near the energy that she had seen Antonio exhibit around the Derby and its aftermath.

All week Isabella turns the incident over in her mind. Was there something that happened during the class? She tries to probe a bit, but Antonio gives no indication of anything wrong. To the contrary, he tells her flat out that he "likes" the class and says "yes" when she asks if he wants to go back. So the next Saturday they go back. And the next. And the next.

## Learning from What Doesn't Work

And then as the next weekend approaches, Antonio is invited to a birthday party to be held at a water park on Saturday. "Can I go, Mommy?" he asks excitedly. "Can I?"

"Well, I don't know about that," Isabella replies. "I mean, don't you remember, you have your horseback riding lesson on Saturdays?"

Antonio pauses. "Oh. Right. Well, can't I just skip this time?"

Isabella starts thinking that this might be a good moment to begin teaching her son about discipline and hard work and making sacrifices to achieve your dreams. "Well, honey, you'll never become a jockey if you don't learn to ride a horse."

Antonio just gives her a blank stare. Then his face wrinkles up as tears fill his eyes and he blurts out, "I know, Mommy. But I want to go to Michael's birthday party!"

And with that, the horseback riding lessons are over.

What has gone wrong? As it turns out, nothing! Nothing at all. Isabella has been quite right to assume that the Kentucky Derby has activated something related to her son's giftedness. And she has also done a fine thing in allowing her aspiring jockey an opportunity to ride some real horses.

Sure, the outcome of that has not at all been what either of them expected. But then, neither has it been a wasted effort. Quite the opposite:

it has shown that whatever it was about the Derby that energized her son, the experience of riding a horse at the stable did not yield him that same energy. Right there is something to pay attention to.

Of course, it's altogether possible that Antonio might take up horseback riding when he is older. Time will tell.

The point is, when you open a door of opportunity for your child and what you think is going to happen doesn't happen, don't chalk that up as a "failure" (either on your part, or even worse, on your child's part). That would be a waste of the moment. Instead, use the experience to learn something about what your child is perhaps *not* motivated to do.

And remember that the wonderful thing about giftedness is that it is irrepressible. That means it can't be stopped. It will bubble up and announce itself over and over and over again, somewhere and somehow. Moreover, as we've already discussed, it is not your responsibility as a parent to make life happen for your child. We've seen parents pour enormous time and resources into their child's "dream," hoping to chaperone them to greatness. The most important thing you can do for your child is help them live well the life they were born to live.

## What About Discipline?

One criticism we sometimes hear in our approach to parenting is that it sounds too permissive for the child. It gives the child too much control over what they want or don't want to do, and what they like and don't like. If you let your child always have their way, the reasoning goes, they'll grow up to be spoiled, entitled people.

> **There's a long tradition that says the goal of discipline is for you as a parent to exert your control over your child.**

We couldn't agree more. But then, we're not at all advocating that you let your child "always have their way." Rather that you parent your child according to The Way of Your Child (as discussed in chapter 5). Those are by no means the same thing, because The Way of Your Child makes a big difference when it comes to discipline.

There's a long tradition that says the goal of discipline is for you as a parent to exert your control over your child. We think that's misguided. We believe that discipline is about using—or better yet, stewarding—your privileged relationship with your child to teach them the importance of self-control. It's about fostering the moral character and integrity of your child. It's not about punishing them for "bad" behavior, but rather forming within them a love and respect for the values that lead them to choose good behavior and healthy relationships, even when doing so comes at a price.

## The Calling Game

When Bev's twin girls were around three or four, they often got so involved in an activity that they didn't respond when their mother called them. Naturally that sort of inattention felt frustrating. In fact, it seemed like a clear-cut case of disobedience. Bev consulted a number of parenting books in search of ways to handle this misbehavior. One of them advised the use of what it called "instant obedience": teach your child that when you call them, they must instantly drop whatever they are doing and rush to obey your orders, or else they'll face certain punishment.

That approach may have suited Captain Von Trapp in *The Sound of Music*, but it was not at all going to work for Bev. In the first place, it would be teaching her girls that she as the mother held all the power. It had nothing to do with getting them to *want* to come to her, but rather everything to do with what would happen if they didn't come. That seemed guaranteed to make them respond only out of fear—hardly the basis for a relationship that should be founded on love and respect and trust, all of which develop character.

In addition, Bev was pretty sure she never wanted her girls to obey anyone indiscriminately. Certainly she wanted to teach them the value of obedience, but in a way that would most effectively make the point. So she turned "when Mommy calls" into a game. She sat them down and told them, "Girls, this weird thing is happening. When I call for you, no one comes! No matter what I need you for—even if I've just made cookies or have a surprise for you—nobody comes! Can you imagine that?"

Then she told them, "I need your help figuring this out. I call and wait for you, but it's as if I never called. Maybe I'm not calling loud enough. Or maybe somebody forgot what to do. But what do you think would help me?"

At that they giggled, and then one of them said, "I'll come, Mommy!" And she got up and ran into the other room and asked Bev to call her.

As soon as Bev called her, she came running back in, and Bev praised her, saying, "You know, that's it! I think we just need to practice this. You guys go in the other room and Mommy will call you, and let's see how you do." And of course, when she called them, they came immediately, laughing and trying to beat each other in getting to their mother.

They practiced the "calling game" several more times, and the girls loved it. Their mother became the person cheering them on, and even when she waited longer intervals before calling them, it was if they couldn't wait to show her they could come.

Then they switched roles and the girls called Bev to come. If she took too much time responding, they would say, "Mommy, you need to practice more!" And by that means, practice became the "discipline." From then on, if Bev ever needed them to respond and they delayed too long, all she had to do to correct them was remind them that they needed extra practice. When they got older, Bev added a small revision to the rule, that if they ever truly needed a couple of minutes to finish something before showing up, they should call out, "Coming!" so that their mother would know they had heard her and were on their way.

Bev also learned an important principle of discipline from that situation. Parents often pay more attention to what their kids are *not* doing than to what they *are* doing. Bev realized she should have been much more curious about what her three-year-olds were doing while she was waiting for them to show up. Something had absorbed their interest—so much so that it was causing them to ignore their mother. What was that fascinating activity? Whatever it was, it quite likely had activated their giftedness.

## Discipline Involves a Relationship

In thinking about discipline, we need to go back to that proverb we looked at in chapter 5:

> Train a child in the way that he should go,
> and when he is old he will not turn from it.

Recall that we said the word translated "train" means to "dedicate" yourself as a parent to guiding and shepherding your child in "the way that your child should go." That underscores how much discipline is about a *relationship*—creating a bond with the heart of your child based on love and loyalty.

While the proverb implies no cause-effect promise, you can rest assured that dedicated parental guidance will teach your child the critical importance of choices—making wise decisions that lead to a life and its behaviors that put things right with the world, including anyone they may have harmed. Judaism calls this *tikkun olam*, or "doing one's part" wherever one goes, performing acts of kindness that repair the world.

## The "Dark Side" of Giftedness

In this book our focus is on giftedness, but we can't stress enough the importance of helping your child develop a character of integrity and moral virtue. That's because while giftedness is inherently good, it is morally neutral. It can be used for good or bad.

The implications of that are far-reaching. The worst things that people do in this world are not the result of their so-called "weaknesses," but rather when they use their core strengths for selfish, misguided, or evil purposes.

- The boy with a gift for numbers and negotiations could grow up to be a brilliant real estate agent who gets the best deal for his clients. But with lack of character he could also grow up to be a con man who swindles senior citizens out of their life savings.

- The girl who loves to meet needs could grow up to be a very attentive, responsive mother whose family's needs are always taken care of. But with lack of character she could also grow up to be a manipulative woman who makes her children so dependent on her that they can't function without her.

Every form of giftedness has a potential "dark side." That's why you want to regularly remind your child that their gift was given to them as a means of loving other people and making a contribution to the world, not to use for their own selfish interests.

## What's Right with This Child?

You will find giftedness everywhere when it comes to discipline. It's in your child. It's in you as their parent. It's in the situation. Let's take these in turn.

First, your child's giftedness will predispose them to behave in ways that may seem out of line or morally suspect to you as their parent. However, please don't automatically label such behaviors as "bad" or "wrong" or "sinful." They may be. But they may not be. They may actually be the best of the child coming out (or trying to come out).

Just imagine for a moment how it is for a small child to possess such big, powerful gifts that have been given them. Our father had a teaching gift like no one we've ever known. It was impossible *not* to respond to his invitation to learn. A former student once described him as "spellbinding." His mother discovered that early on. So when they rode the streetcars in Philadelphia in the 1920s, she would push little Howard forward whenever they had to interact with other people. Years later he described how he could tell even then that he had a way with people—and it actually felt a little scary because he realized it gave him a kind of power over others.

**The more powerful a child's gifts are, the more driven the child is to express them—some way, somehow.**

The more powerful a child's gifts are, the more driven the child is to express them—some way, somehow. Those first attempts so often squirt out sideways for a little one who, at that age, is naturally impulsive and still lacks for resources in terms of language, appropriate behavior, discernment, etc. for using their gifts well.

So in light of that, your job as a parent is not to shut down the behavior (inappropriate though it may be), even less to shame them for being precisely the person they are. Rather, you want to help them learn how to be the *best* of that person by making good choices and gaining skill in stewarding well all that they've been given.

Again, we grant that the behavior may seem puzzling, or frustrating, or oppositional, or angering, or otherwise upsetting *to* you. But that's where your giftedness comes into the relationship. The child may be doing nothing "wrong," nonetheless you're troubled because it's not what you would do, since you have a different giftedness. Remember what we've said about, "What's wrong with you?!" You'll certainly feel like saying that, at times. But if you're wise, you'll press "Mute" on that put-down and instead concentrate on answering the opposite question: "What's *right* with this child whom I love with all my heart? How can I reframe this situation and see what they *are* doing, and recognize the gift of that?" And moreover, call them to a more constructive use for that impulse.

## The Be-in-Charge Child

A telling example of how this works is the child who is born to control things and be in charge. There is absolutely nothing wrong with that form of giftedness. Indeed, people born with that motivation often grow up to be strong leaders in government, the military, business and industry, education, and other institutions of society. That's good because every enterprise needs somebody to be in charge. Why not someone who is uniquely gifted to that task?

But suppose that long before that be-in-charge person is named CEO, or wins her wings as a fighter pilot, or finally gets elected to office, or gets promoted to Chief of Police, they are a three-year-old be-in-charge toddler growing up in your household with you as their parent.

You'll likely see signs of their giftedness very early on. Perhaps even as an infant you noticed something very aware and commanding about their expressions, something in the insistence of their crying, something in the way they negotiated bathtimes, bedtimes, and every "no" you said to them, something in their play that showed a certain forcefulness or aggression. At times it was almost like they had a chip on their shoulder. But then, in the next minute, they might have changed into a real charmer.

Now, as a preschooler, just getting them dressed for the day can be a knock-down, drag-out battle! Nor is there any rhyme or reason. One day they insist on the blue socks, the next day it must be the red ones, the next it is no socks at all. When you try to explain that it's fifteen degrees outside and they *must* wear some warm socks, you're likely to be met with a temper tantrum loud enough to have the neighbors calling Child Protective Services.

Mealtimes are even worse. The peas must be completely separated from the mashed potatoes, or else they will not be tolerated. Somehow, every time you turn your back the sippy cup keeps landing on the floor. And when you tell your toddler there will be no dessert until they have finished their dinner, they sit defiantly and indefinitely, their plate remaining untouched.

## "What's Wrong with You?!"

Few parents can withstand the temptation to react to such behavior by thinking or saying, "What's wrong with you?!" Many of those parents will further conclude that their child's defiant behavior is an open-and-shut case for disciplining them.

Indeed, you can find plenty of advice out there for handling what is called the "strong-willed child." Much of it is well intended, though some of it harshly recommends that you must break your child's will or spirit—something we would never recommend because you would only end up breaking your child. That's exactly what you don't want to do.

If one perceives the purpose of parenting as staying in control over your child, then raising a be-in-charge child automatically turns the parent-child relationship into a battle. To win, the parent has to stay in control. But that means the child must lose. How do you suppose a child-person who is hard-wired to make sure they end up in charge is going to feel when they consistently lose the control and must subordinate themselves to someone more powerful than they are? It will not turn out to be a pretty picture!

That's why we're advocating an altogether different approach to parenting. We assert that the purpose of parenting is to guide the infant person you have been given into their adult person, according to Your Child's Way. In this case, Your Child's Way involves a giftedness for gaining control and exercising power.

So what is your job as that child's parent? In sum, it is (a) begin to recognize this little one's gift (you've already started to do that, as we've seen); (b) begin to honor that gift—even at such a tender age—by cooperating with it and giving it opportunities for expression; (c) help your child take their first steps in learning to manage their gift and exercise it appropriately; and (d) celebrate your child and their gift by developing positive language to affirm them and help them (as well as you) begin to discover the value of the powerful gift they've been given.

When you look at things that way, the battle of the wills largely goes away. And let's be honest, was there—is there, can there ever be—ever any serious question of "who is in charge" between a three-year-old and their parent? With the exception of the child's giftedness, the parent holds all the cards: physical strength, knowledge about how the world works, authority over the housing, the food, the money, the schedule, and countless other factors.

## Give Them Something to Control

Growing up in the midst of such a power differential, your three-year-old, be-in-charge tyke is simply asking a pretty natural and obvious question: *What can I find around here that I can be in charge of? What can I impose my will on?* That seems like a fair question, given their makeup. Why not help them find answers to it?

For instance:

- "So you're saying you want to wear your red socks today instead of your blue ones? Well, the red ones haven't been through the laundry yet, but if that's your decision, let's go with it."

- "What, no socks today? Surely not! Come outside with me. Feel how cold it is! It's freezing! Are your feet getting cold? Yeah! Brrrr! What are you going to do to keep your feet warm with it being this cold?"

- "Hmmm, so those four peas can't get eaten because they touched the mashed potatoes? Is that the rule? Okay, I'll tell you what. Here are four peas on my plate that haven't touched the mashed potatoes. See? They followed the rule. So here, I'm going to give you these four peas, and I'll take the ones from your plate that didn't follow the rule. You eat my four and then I can eat your four, and it'll all be good, okay. Ready?" (Hey, it might work and it might not, but it leaves the kid with a degree of control.)

- "So I see you've decided not to finish 'this much' of your dinner and just skip dessert? You're sure about that? That's how you want to leave it? Okay, then, now that we've finished supper, show me what you were putting together in your room today." (Somewhere there must be a rulebook that says children *must* finish all of their dinner every single night, but we've never seen that book. But you know, hunger has an amazing way of bending a child's will to its demands. For example, meals the following day may look far more appealing after skipping the rest of dinner the night before. And there's always the possibility that a little while after dinner, your child will ask, "If I finish my dinner now, can I have some dessert?" In that case, you've both "won.")

Notice that the important thing in all of this is not winning or beating them at their game. Rather it's you helping your be-in-control child learn to contain and develop the emotional muscle they'll need to work with the immensity of power that is propelling them to insist on having their own way all the time.

## The Power of the Positive

Sometimes you have no choice but to enforce your will over your child's will, no matter how much they dislike it. But in the preschool years—as with all the years thereafter—you have to pick your battles carefully.

The point is to never punish your child for being who they are. Yes, let them experience consequences for expressing themselves in hurtful or inappropriate ways. But learn to get in the habit of stepping back and looking at the *person* contained in the little body in front of you, and ask (with discernment rather than judgment): What is my child telling me about themselves? What sorts of strengths and motivation might be driving this behavior that I'm seeing? What aspects of their personhood may be getting frustrated or blocked, thereby causing this behavior?

**Never punish your child for being who they are.**

We've already mentioned the way in which parents and others start to assign labels to behavior they perceive as odd or out of the ordinary. This is especially so when a child pushes the boundaries of what is right and wrong, good and bad.

Again, how your child expresses themselves may indeed be wrong or inappropriate or hurtful. As the parent, it's your job to help them define and defend boundaries. Doing so actually helps your child feel secure, even though they may pitch a fit. But even in doing so, our appeal is to always look for what they are doing (or trying to do) right, and to end up developing positive language to acknowledge that. In other words, how might you reinterpret "bad" behavior into a positive affirmation of your child's strengths?

So, to return to the be-in-charge three-year-old above: it is wrong for the youngster to have pushed baby sister so forcefully in the rocker that she fell out and is now screaming her lungs out on the floor. Understandably, all the protective instincts in you as a mother are to lash out at your child and send them off crying to their room while you scoop up the baby and start calming her down.

But as you do so, you also have an opportunity to reframe what has just happened. Which means trying to see what happened through the eyes of your three-year-old, not just yours. Obviously as a parent, you're wondering, *What were they thinking?* But that's kind of the real question, isn't it: What were *they* thinking? How were *they* approaching the situation, even despite its unpleasant outcome?

If you're already aware that your toddler consistently shows a tendency toward taking the upper hand, exerting their will on things (sometimes forcefully), and wanting things to go their way, then you have the beginnings of an answer to that question: *What were they thinking?*

Later, after baby has nodded off and (hopefully) calm has settled over the home once again, you can go to your preschooler and have a conversation about the incident. Perhaps something along these lines:

"Honey, your sister could have been hurt very badly by falling out of the rocker like that. Tell me what happened."

"I didn't mean to hurt her, Mommy. She just fell out."

"Well, she fell out because you were pushing her too hard. You have to be gentle with babies. Can you tell me what happened?"

"Well, you were on the phone, and I thought I could help you out by taking care of Lisa. She had stopped rocking, and she was starting to cry. I know that upsets you when she cries, so I thought I would rock her to keep her from doing that. Then she just fell out."

"I see. Well, you're a big helper to do that for Mommy when she's busy doing something else. I love that about you, that you're always thinking about ways to be a helper and a leader. Thank you for being that way! And after today, you can see that when you help Mommy with Lisa, you have to be real gentle with her because she's just a baby. Think of it like you're there to protect her and keep her safe, as well as to make her happy. Can you do that?"

Affirming your child's strengths—even when they get expressed inappropriately—is so important and so powerful during the preschool years. Because very soon your child is going to enter a wider world, called school. In that world, their unique behavior will not always be beloved by others. Sadly, it's a world where negative labels and hurtful misperceptions abound. So you want to infuse your youngster ahead of time with a confidence that even though they sometimes do bad things, they have inherent worth as a person, and that there's a certain way they have of being in the world that is *just right*.

# PART III

## education

# 9

# school daze

In this section we want to talk about the implications of giftedness for your child's education. A whole book could be written on that because parents today are confronted by countless opinions about how their children should be educated. We're not the experts to help you sort out all those options. But here's what we can tell you with absolute confidence: no matter what sort of schooling your child receives, their individual giftedness remains the key indicator of the way they will learn best and how they will respond to any particular educational setting.

## What's the "Best" School?

Right off the bat, that means that as you evaluate where your child will attend school, you should investigate the extent to which that school makes it a priority to serve different kinds of learners, and if so, what that looks like. Some families have options for where to send their child to school, while others don't. Either way, the "best" school for your child is a school where their uniqueness is taken into account.

If you've been paying attention in your child's early years, by the time they start school you should have some idea about how they respond in learning situations. So the issue is not that there is only one place that can educate your child well, but rather, where is the best fit in terms of what you value as a family and where your child is most likely to thrive in learning?

And by the way, there's absolutely no need to stress out about where your child gets started in school. Doing so would be taking a Child-As-a-Product approach to parenting—you know, the one that says if you send your kid to the "right" schools, they'll turn out "right."

**Some families have options for where to send their child to school, while others don't. Either way, the "best" school for your child is a school where their uniqueness is taken into account.**

That's silly. Certainly you should think carefully about your child's education—whether public school, private school, homeschool, or some combination thereof. But no matter how hard you try to figure things out ahead of time, it's going to be the real-life experiences of school that reveal the most important factors about your child's learning.

Remember . . . your child is not a product, but a *person*. The purpose of education is not to "make" them into someone, but rather to facilitate their development in terms of what they are born to do. In that case, the ultimate, core question for which every parent and teacher ought to be seeking an answer is: *What is this child born to do, and how does that affect the learning process for them?*

## Learning Styles

In recent years, educators have started paying attention to the fact that children display a variety of what might be called "learning styles." Quite simply, different children learn in different ways.

We couldn't agree more. Only instead of trying to classify children according to, say, four, or seven, or ten, or sixteen, or however many "categories" or "types" of learning styles there supposedly are, we prefer to simply say that every child is unique in how they learn. That follows from the idea that every person is unique—as in, one of a kind. Yes, two individuals may have much in common, but in the end they are distinct, unique persons.

We could show you the giftedness assessments of thousands and thousands of people from more than half a century of research to back up that claim. Those descriptions would show, for example, that while one person *must* have a personal, one-on-one interaction with a teacher or guide to thrive as a learner, someone else learns best on their own, with no teacher needed. One person learns best in team-oriented activities, while another needs to work independently. Some learners absorb information by listening to a talk, others by reading a book, others by having an experience, still others by figuring things out on the fly. Some people thrive in structured, classroom settings; others gain more through unstructured activities.

## Becoming Your Child's Advocate

Different people learn in different ways, based on the dynamics of their unique giftedness. That reality leads to the obvious implication that, ideally, your child should be placed in the learning environment that best suits their particular learning style.

But alas, that's easier said than done. For one thing, if your child is just starting school, you may not yet know much about their learning style (although hopefully you've been making observations as we've suggested and recording them in your child's giftedness journal, as described in Chapter 6). Another reality is that your options may be limited. Sure, in a big city you can probably find a private school that emphasizes customized learning. But you may not live in a big city, and you may not be able to afford such a school even if you do.

Furthermore, no matter where you end up placing your child for their early education, every school is set up to optimize its particular approach to education. In other words, every school dispenses their instruction in a certain way, according to their chosen educational philosophy. Even public schools tend to standardize their approach across a district, with perhaps a few magnet schools or charter schools thrown in with their particular spins on education. Hopefully you can find an approach that somewhat overlaps with how your child best learns. But where there's not an overlap, it's almost always going to be your child who will have to accommodate herself to the school's educational approach rather than the school trying to fit itself to your child's learning style.

If you've been educated in the traditional way, you've already experienced how that works. You know that academic settings tend to work well for people who learn by reading, writing, memorizing, thinking conceptually, and taking tests. And sitting still. But what if someone learns in other ways? Then they'll tend to struggle in academic learning environments. They won't do as well as their peers who have more of that "academic" style of learning.

That's bad enough. But on top of that, academic settings rate students' performance using a system called "grades." The people who learn well (because their learning style matches the instructional method) get the better grades. Those who don't learn so well (because of a learning/instruction mismatch) get the lesser grades. Over time, whether the system intends it or not, the students who get the better grades are perceived to be the "smart" people, while those who get the lesser grades are seen as "not smart."

Yet nothing could be further from the truth! When you place those "not smart" students in other learning environments—for example, on a basketball court, on a track team, in a band, in a theater production, in an art class, in a community service project, in an investment club, on a wilderness expedition, in a cross-cultural immersion experience, later on out in the work world—suddenly their performance goes off the charts! They can look brilliant. That's because their giftedness has finally encountered circumstances that favor how they learn and develop.

Look, we have nothing against academic settings. We ourselves did well in those learning environments. But we can't stress enough that not everyone thrives in those settings. So when it comes to your child, you as the parent must become an advocate on behalf of your child. Your role is to do what you can to make whatever schooling your child is in work as best as possible for them, given their unique giftedness.

**You can't just hand over your child to a school with the attitude, "You're the experts. Here, take my child and educate them."**

You can't just hand over your child to a school with the attitude, "You're the experts in education. Here, take my child and educate them." Yes, the schools are supposed to be experts in education, but *you are the expert (or should be) on your child*—especially if you've already got four or five or more years of observations from your child's lived experience about how they engage the world. That insight alone gives you the right to work with the school in tailoring its expertise to help your child learn as well as they can in that setting.

## Working with Your Child's Teachers

"Working with the school," of course, really means working with your child's teachers. Bev taught middle-school English for several years before raising three daughters of her own. So she brings experience from both sides of that parent-teacher relationship. She recalls that as a teacher, working with parents was one of her favorite parts of the job. She saw it as a partnership because she knew that in order for her work with a child to thrive, she had to get their parents on board.

Many teachers are gifted to the task of teaching, while unfortunately others are not. Regardless, we believe most teachers want to do a good job. So if you as a parent take that as a given, the relationship will begin in a good place. You definitely should make it a priority to get to know your child's teachers and extend them your respect and support in every way you can. After all, they're going to have a considerable influence on your child.

We as parents are tempted to assume that we automatically know what's best when it comes to our child. But the reality is that a good teacher often sees or picks up on things we don't see because they have the benefit of observing our child in a school setting. They also bring a degree of objectivity that can be quite helpful.

You don't have to agree with everything your child's teacher tells you, but at least hear them out and carefully consider their input—again with respect and appreciation for their perspective. Also, keep in mind that most of today's teachers are under incredible pressures and being asked to do far more than their compensation or training account for. By granting them a degree of empathy for all they are responsible for, you increase the likelihood that you and they will form a strong working relationship.

So what if you sense that something going on in the classroom is adverse to your child's success and needs to be addressed? By all means, address it! Always pay attention when your child is not happy or feeling unsuccessful at school—for whatever reasons. As their advocate, you need to show up for them. That doesn't mean to go on the attack. It means you use the same voice of respect and support to gather all the information you can from the teacher in order to sort out what seems to be happening and what can be done about it. In the end, what matters most is what your child learns from how *you* handle a challenging situation.

Your job is to stay plugged in to what is going on in your child's educational experience and advocate for your student's best as much as you can. You may feel you have no choice, for instance, about sending them to the public school down the street, but you always have a choice about how conscientious you are about making it a priority to know what goes on for your child in whatever school environment they happen to have. Getting involved in the PTA, responding to volunteer requests when possible, showing up with interest and openness for parent conferences, looking over homework and providing appropriate support for school projects all put you on the front lines to be aware of problems as they are developing and give you credibility, if and when you feel you need to address issues with the administration and staff. Remember, by paying attention over the years to the developing giftedness of your child, you bring so much to that conversation, serving as not only the parent, but also an invested champion of the person called Your Child.

# 10

# setting expectations

Parents vary widely in terms of how well they expect their children to do at school. Some parents demand straight As. Others are pleased as long as their kids bring home mostly Bs and Cs. Others, sadly, don't really care one way or the other about how well or how poorly their children do at school.

But whether parents set the expectations high, low, or somewhere in between, they all too often make the mistake of failing to factor the giftedness of their child into the equation. Yet that's what makes all the difference because, as we said earlier, giftedness is the trump card in the whole educational process. Let's look at some ways for how that works.

## Calibrate your expectations to fit your child.

In evaluating your child's performance, whose interests are you putting first—your own or your child's? Don't be too quick to answer that! Remember, we live in a culture that says a child is a product, which means the performance of a child is a direct reflection on the child's parents. When a child does well in school, their parents get a round of applause.

But if a child does poorly, the parents hang their heads in shame.

"But I just want my child to do well in school," a parent will say. That's fine. Most of us as parents want our children to thrive as they learn and grow. But there's a world of difference between saying "I want my child to do well in school in terms of developing into who they were born to be" and "I want my child to do well in school in order to make me look good as a parent."

Let's go back to what we said earlier about grades. Grades are the designated metric of academic settings. Whether they're the best metric is arguable, but by no means should they be the only metric. If they are, then some children will quickly figure out how to game the system and make great grades, but never really learn the subjects. By the same token, if grades are all that matter, then some kids will get defeated and demotivated easily when they don't get the grades that were expected of them or that they expected of themselves.

**In our experience, most kids don't grow up setting their sights too high, but too low.**

By virtue of their giftedness, some children do well in academic settings; others do not. For that reason, we think it's better to emphasize effort and growth over measuring up to some comparative standard. That means affirming your child for doing their best, even in subjects that are hard, and praising them for showing tenacity and resilience, no matter what the final grade turns out to be.

### Your child needs a vision for their life.

As you know by now, we believe every child was placed here for a purpose. Your child will be the rest of their life discovering their purpose. But from their earliest days, they need to be made aware that they even *have* a purpose. That awareness will transform their experience in school because it connects school with a much larger vision for their life.

Popular myth holds that Americans think boldly and dream big dreams. But that's not always what we've seen. In our experience, most kids don't grow up setting their sights too high, but too low. In large part, that's because they don't know what their giftedness is, so they have no idea of their potential. But it's also because no one has ever challenged them to think about their future and what they might do with their life. In the absence of that sort of vision casting, most teens and young adults will default to the uninspiring task of "just getting a job." Or worse.

As a parent, you can play an invaluable role in helping your child believe that they were put here for a purpose. Yes, they'll need to earn a living. But your child needs to start dreaming about a vision for their life. A vision is a picture of what their life could look like in ten or twenty or even thirty years if they apply themselves to developing their strengths and giving them every opportunity to take flight.

Obviously this is going to be a work in progress. Some children are very concrete in the way they are wired, so the idea of a "vision" may be far too abstract for them to immediately grasp. In that case, look for concrete illustrations of the idea of growth over time, things that your child can see or experience. So for example, you might have them choose a plant to grow in the backyard and then guide them through all the necessary steps for making that a reality—buying the seeds, preparing the soil, reading about watering and feeding the plant, setting a schedule for maintaining it.

In helping them dream, however, make sure that the future they begin to envision is actually *their* vision, not your agenda for their life. You may think they have the potential to play in the NFL, but let *them* resolve to pursue that dream. Don't force it on them. Likewise, you may be a doctor or a teacher in a long line of physicians or educators, but don't lock your child into the idea that it's their destiny as one of the family to follow that same career path.

## Most of your child's development will take place in their areas of giftedness.

Your child's giftedness will never fundamentally change, but that doesn't mean they won't grow and develop. They absolutely will! But their most dynamic growth will be according to their areas of giftedness. That has some definite implications for setting expectations.

For one thing, it means they should focus on their strengths. Does your child show an aptitude for arithmetic and math? Then encourage them in arithmetic and math. Do they respond to that encouragement by doing even more arithmetic and math? Then feed that energy with even more encouragement. Find opportunities for them to expand their activities around arithmetic and math. Show them how you keep the family budget and let them start helping you with that. Track down brain teasers, games, and other problem-solving exercises involving arithmetic and math. If they seem to want even more arithmetic and math, then find them a tutor (if you can afford one) to take them even further into ever-higher levels of arithmetic and math.

In other words, always devote the most energy and resources to your child's strengths and areas of motivated interest.

The one caveat to keep in mind is that their interests can change. Not their giftedness, mind you, but how they express it. Bev recalls a client whose parents were always one hundred percent behind whatever she was interested in. She told the story of how, as a young girl, she loved to do craft projects. So they piled on the craft kits at every birthday and Christmas and on other special occasions.

But as it turned out, while this woman enjoyed opportunities to be creative and work on projects from beginning to end, her giftedness was fundamentally about who else was involved with her in a given activity. What mattered, motivationally speaking, was the participation with another person, not what they were doing together.

It was this woman's beloved grandmother who first invited her to do a craft project with her. And that was the joy—doing it with her Nana. By contrast, if she was alone in her room, doing some craft project just didn't feel very motivating. But then she began to feel guilty because her parents had bought her countless kits that she felt obligated to finish. She didn't have the heart to tell them that she had moved on to other areas of interest.

One takeaway from this woman's experience is the importance of asking your child what *they* enjoy about an activity they seem to love. It's so easy to assume that once they latch onto an activity, *eureka!* This is "their thing," and now you know what their giftedness is. But as always, the giftedness is in the child, not in the activity. So stay alert to new avenues of interest and expression.

And let the child, not you, drive the energy for a particular activity. The woman who received all the craft kits from her parents deeply appreciated their encouragement. But she made the observation that "sometimes it felt like it was too much. It almost seemed as if *they* were more into everything I ever showed interest in than I was." That's quite revealing! Even with all your best intentions, it's possible to overpower your child's voice with your own energy and enthusiasm.

> **The absence of a strength is merely a limitation—what someone is *not* designed to do.**

## But what about weaknesses?

"But what about my child's weaknesses?" someone will ask. "What do I do about them?" The short answer is twofold: (1) stop labeling them as weaknesses; and (2) don't pay so much attention to them.

What exactly is a "weakness"? One definition describes it as a lack of strength. That we can accept. The absence of a strength is merely a limitation—what someone is *not* designed to do. But a common perception of a *weakness* is that it's a flaw, fault, or defect. That negative cast is never going to be helpful for a child.

Look at it this way: a pen is designed to write. We would say it has a strength for writing, and if you use it for that purpose, it works brilliantly. But we would never say to the pen, "You know, you do a great job at writing, but you have a real weakness when it comes to opening paint cans." No! If we need that job done, we go get a tool that has the strength (or giftedness) to do that task.

We never describe tools as having a weakness, but we do that all the time with people. We tell them what they don't do well, but in doing so, we fail to consider what they are designed to do, what they are born to do.

Some people are born to work with numbers. Others aren't. Maybe they're born to work with words. Or with bugs. Or with music. Or with machinery. Or with people. Or with theories.

So as you set expectations for your son or daughter, figure out what *they* appear to be born to work with, and have them focus on that. As for their limitations (meaning the areas in which they lack natural strengths), just encourage them to do the best they can in those areas. If it's a skill or knowledge base that they really must acquire (e.g., the times tables or the spelling of words), help them figure out how they can work "smarter" at that area by using their strengths. For instance, maybe they don't memorize well by themselves, but they do better if they can work together with you to come up with a system that helps them remember.

In the end, doing "the best they can" may result in better grades, but then again it may not. They may end up doing only passingly well, if that.

Is that okay? That's for you and your child to decide. But consider this: Albert Einstein excelled when he started school, but he came to loathe the teaching style of his instructors, which relied on rote memory and rigid discipline. So he dropped out at fifteen. Then he flunked the entrance exam for a polytechnic institute in Zurich, having passed the math portion but failed the botany, zoology, and language sections. He tried again the next year and passed, but he struggled all the way through the institute and barely graduated.[1]

Does anyone ever ask why Einstein didn't apply himself more in botany, zoology, and language (his so-called "weakest" subjects)? Of course not! If anything, one wonders why the schools (let alone his parents) never noticed that he was particularly adept at math and therefore, never encouraged his efforts in that direction.

Remember, giftedness is not just about strength or ability; it's also about *intrinsic* motivation, the energy that comes from within. Intrinsic motivation is a form of desire. That's why the best learning—the learning that lasts—is not driven by one's head, but by one's heart.

## Some forms of giftedness show themselves in performance or achievement. Other giftedness looks quite different.

Parents ought to take that into account as they set expectations for their children's schoolwork. But alas, as we've said, they rarely do. Case in point:

For as long as her parents can remember, Jenna has been fiercely competitive. Whether playing games, riding bikes, doing chores, memorizing vocabulary lists, selling Girl Scout cookies, or auditioning for school plays, Jenna is determined to come out on top. Not surprisingly, Jenna applies that winning spirit at school when it comes to grades. She not only keeps track of her own test scores, assignment grades, and other metrics that go into the grading system, she figures out ways to monitor where the other students in her classes likely stand, so that she knows who she has to "beat."

By contrast, Jenna's younger brother, Oliver, could care less about winning or losing. He spent the better part of his preschool years leafing through the picture books that his sister used to look at before she graduated to "real" books. Often he would pull out some paper and crayons and try to draw the colorful things he saw in the books. He liked re-creating the shapes and colors. For that matter, he also liked the "feel" of drawing and coloring—the texture of the paper, the smooth, waxy consistency of the crayons, the relaxing rhythm in his hand as he shaded in the various images. He could draw for hours.

But of course, that's all changed now that Oliver is in elementary school. Now he has schedules to follow, rules to remember, materials and supplies he has to keep track of, assignments he must complete, and even a bit of homework to do at night. It all feels a little over-whelming to him. Frankly, a lot of it doesn't even make sense to him. So Oliver just ignores much of his schoolwork.

Instead, he has taken to playing an old piano in the basement. Like the drawings he did as a small child, he loves the experience of the piano and the way he can create pictures with music, or even tell little stories through sound. He discovers endless possibilities for what he can do through his fingers as they become ever more familiar with the black and white piano keys.

## Delight or Disappointment?

Now we should tell you that these children's parents are both college graduates who also have master's degrees. They place a high value on achievement, applying oneself, and taking responsibility. You can probably imagine, then, what happens every six weeks during the school year when their children bring home their report cards from school.

Jenna can't wait to show her list of straight As to her parents—usu-ally with some commentary like, "Zoe Williams and Jason Lee made straight As, too. But Jason was five points behind me, and I managed to beat Zoe by one point."

"That's fantastic, Jen!" exclaims her father. "Way to go! You really deserve these grades. You worked so hard these past six weeks. I'm so proud of you!"

Then there's a pause, and Dad finally asks, "Oliver, where's your report card?"

Oliver looks puzzled for a moment, then says, "Oh, right. Let me go get it." A moment later he returns with the form and hands it to his father, who opens it up and gives it the once-over. The father's expression at that point says everything that needs to be said. Once again, Oliver has disappointed his parents' expectations.

So what's to be done in a situation like this? The options generally boil down to three. One is for Oliver's parents to tighten the screws on their expectations for him. Maybe that will help. Let's make him do his homework at the kitchen table, where we can watch to make sure he's studying, not goofing off. Let's find him a tutor to help him focus more on the subjects he's doing poorly in. Why, let's get rid of that stupid piano. *That's* the problem! And let's take him to get tested for a learning disability. Surely we can figure this out and turn things around! We know plenty of parents who have opted for that double-down strategy. It almost never turns out well.

Other parents choose instead to simply keep their mouths shut, to ignore the situation. Maybe even go into denial about it. Does that work any better? Not much. Parents may be able to hold their tongue, but it's awfully hard to hide their feelings. Yet a child can always feel emotional detachment. And they will likely turn that into a narrative along the lines of, "My parents don't really care. They never ask about school or show any interest in what I like to do. It's like I'm furniture that nobody really notices. I wonder if they even love me."

The third option is for the parents to notice that their expectations are just that—*their* expectations, not their child's. And then recalibrate those expectations in line with the Way of Their Child. That is, with the observations they have made about what brings their son or daughter energy—what they appear to be born to do.

In Oliver's case, his parents would do well to accept that he may never be inclined to excel in academic subjects. He's clearly a creative child who lives for the experience of making something new and conceptually appealing. And unfortunately, the way most academic subjects are taught in many schools will fail to motivate him. Where is the place he might be able to shine at school? As his advocates, his parents need to find out.

They may not find an abundance of such opportunities, but they should seek out what they can. Maybe they hear about an art or music class. Maybe they talk to a social studies teacher and learn about an upcoming project that calls for making a poster or some other visual display. Perhaps an English teacher who seems sympathetic agrees to let Oliver compose a jingle for an assignment instead of just writing a poem, like the other students. Or maybe his parents explain the situation to a music teacher who then agrees to show Oliver some techniques for playing the piano, along with his first steps in music theory.

## The Best Version of Your Child

The aim is to give Oliver some oxygen in an environment where otherwise he's suffocating, motivationally speaking. He hasn't done anything wrong. Nor has the school. It's simply a mismatch between what a child inclines toward and how his school is set up to operate.

As for the various subjects that don't interest him, Oliver's parents should encourage him, as we said earlier, to do "the best he can." In the vast majority of educational settings, that's a low bar, because if he'll just give it even a little bit of effort, he'll pass 99 percent of his homework and courses. Only the kids who do *nothing* are failed.

At best, school may always be something of a "can do" rather than a "love to do" for Oliver. But where his parents can really get behind him is when the school day ends. Now the options open up for really fanning the flames of Oliver's strengths and interests. So don't get rid of the piano, trade it in for a newer, better piano. If lessons would help (they might or might not, depending on how Oliver learns), then find the right teacher. Does Oliver still like to draw? Then get him some decent pencils and sketchpads. Commission him to render a drawing for a grandparent's birthday. Take him to art galleries. Take him to concerts. Introduce him to working artists and musicians, people who speak his language. See if he wants to pick up other instruments besides the piano. See if he wants to expand into sculpture or pottery or leatherwork or painting. Invite him to be creative in the kitchen if he wants, and see what he cooks up.

**At best, school may always be something of a "can do" rather than a "love to do" for kids like Oliver.**

You get the idea. In setting expectations for your own Oliver, the most important expectation of all is this: "Oliver, no matter what else, I always want you to be the best version of *you*. I don't know all that that means yet, but when I look at you, I see a boy who loves to draw and make music and bring creative expressions to life. I *love* that about you! And that's what I want you to do your best at, okay? Yes, I want you to try hard in arithmetic and spelling and reading group and the rest of it. But where I know you can shine is in the creative stuff. So that's what I'm going to be looking for—all those wonderful Oliver creations you come up with!"

# 11

# homework

I n the last chapter we talked about calibrating your expectations for your child's performance in school according to their unique "bent" or Way. Much of that also applies to how you help them approach their homework.

And when we say "homework," we really do mean *home*-work, that is, schoolwork that your child brings home to be done in the home environment. That's a great opportunity to observe *how* they approach that work. If you pay attention, you'll notice that certain factors may enhance or limit their success at that task.

Whatever you do, especially with your elementary or middle school child, don't just tell them, "Go do your homework!" Instead, show some interest and curiosity about what they've been assigned to do, even if they've proven to be fairly independent and responsible about their homework. Showing them you care emphasizes the importance of learning, and it may lead to some new insights about what interests and motivates them.

**Whatever you do, don't just tell them, "Go do your homework!"**

Here are some pointers for "helping with homework."

## Pay attention to your child's preferred way of tackling assignments.

Homework is (among other things) a handoff of a task between a teacher and a student. It's not much different than what happens in the work world when a manager gives an assignment to an employee. What giftedness shows is that people differ widely on how they want that handoff to take place and what they need to succeed once they are given their marching orders. When your child is given homework, here are four possibilities (there are others) for how they might receive it, based on their particular giftedness:

- *"Tell me what I'm supposed to do and then leave me alone while I go do it. I will ask for help if I need it."* This is the independent student who prefers to study alone. That makes things pretty easy on a parent. When it's time to do homework, their child goes off by themself and gets after it.

- *"Give me plenty of orientation up front about what this is about and how it works and what is expected of me. Then I'll go work on it."* In giving out homework, a teacher needs to clarify exactly what is being asked of the student and how the assignment works. Some of that orientation might take place during class, the rest of it could be handled by some sort of introduction in the homework itself.

    That's how things should happen. But unfortunately that's not always the case. So here's where a parent can help. Pay attention if your child has a hard time getting started on their homework, or if they show difficulty in getting traction on it. The truth is, they may not understand what they're supposed to do or how the assignment works. You might help by reviewing the instructions yourself to clarify what they mean, then explaining them so that your child understands. You should also have them reach out to the teacher to get clarification. That shows them the importance of asking for help when they need it. It also signals to the teacher that for some students the instructions being given about the homework may need to be fleshed out a bit more.

- *"Show me how this works, and then I'll get started. But I need you to be available if I have questions or get stuck."* Students in this category probably get overlooked more than any other because parents are often busy doing other things while their child is struggling with their homework. Unless a parent has made it clear that their child can interrupt them at any time, the child may not want to "bother" mom or dad with "some silly question about my stupid homework."

What's often going on here is that the child's giftedness requires lots of reassurance that they are on the right track and meeting expectations, and that they can get needed input if they are off course. The child legitimately wants to get it right, but in the absence of someone from the outside being available to help them, they can easily get stuck.

And why not, because how many of us get something right the first time we try it? Learning is all about trying new things, which means the highway to competence leads directly through incompetence. So that means lots of mistakes and the freedom to make them. As the parent, you can be the voice of encouragement your child may need to keep building that bridge between, "This is not working and I don't know what to do," and the other side, which says, "Okay, now I'm getting the hang of it, and things are going much better. Maybe I can actually do this after all."

By the way, it never helps a child to just tell them, "You need to do this yourself." That's especially the case if you're trying to push them to become more independent. When your child asks you questions, they are accessing their lifeline. The last thing you want to do is cut that off in any way. There are many ways to encourage independence in children, but most often it involves a staged process in which the child feels supported as they gain competence and confidence over time.

- *"Don't ask me to do this by myself. I need to do this with a partner or a team. Who can I work with?"* For some reason, studying and homework have always been regarded as activities one should do alone. But it turns out that the vast majority of people function best as part of a team, or at least in partnership with another person. That suggests that many students would actually study better and learn more if they teamed up with others.

   That's a controversial idea, we admit. What's to keep a group of seventh graders from straying off-topic into wasting time? How can the essentially identical homework turned in by two students who have worked together possibly reflect individual performance? And isn't it only a matter of time before students learn to game this system by grouping up with the kids who know all the answers or will be most likely to do all the work, and just like that everyone gets an A?

   Those are challenges, to be sure. Our point is that many students do *not* work well by themselves, and if they are forced to do so, they will likely turn in a lackluster performance at best. That's one major reason why the academic parts of schooling are so often demotivating for many, because students are forced to do many activities as individuals rather than as part of a team.

   You and your child will have to decide what's best for them as they tackle their homework. But if you see your child struggling to get started on their homework or to stick with it, or if you see them rushing through their homework with a superficial, "let's get this over with" attitude, and you know by experience that they thrive when they collaborate with others—you might experiment with a bit of group homework. Put some safeguards in place to make sure actual homework is getting done and everyone is contributing fairly. But you might be doing your child a favor. In fact, you might be showing them a study strategy that they'll need later in college.

## Provide structure if your child needs it.

By "structure" we mean a game plan, a strategy for how your child will devote their energy to their homework assignments.

By now it should be abundantly clear that some people excel in bringing structure and planning to their efforts, while others do not. Some people set goals. Some make schedules. Some create timelines or even charts of their progress. Others are much more laid back. We saw that with Oliver, the creative child who could care less about where he's supposed to be at a given time. He's not about "getting anywhere." He is wired to stick with a creative moment for as long as it remains conceptually interesting.

If your child is a planner who plots out what assignments they have to complete and by when, you're good to go as a parent. All you have to do is periodically monitor their progress and help them keep on track.

But what if your child is more like Oliver? Or what if they chronically misjudge the time they need and seem to end up waiting until the last possible minute to cram and stay up late to get an assignment done? Or what if they just get so distracted by their sport or their ballet lessons or their friends that they just "forget" when things are due?

There's nothing wrong with any of these children for being "unstructured." Their giftedness doesn't need them to be structured. Indeed, it requires that they remain fairly unstructured. But that puts them at a disadvantage in an academic setting where there is structure, like assignments and deadlines and expectations and metrics for success.

Instead of criticizing them for being "irresponsible" or "lazy" or "forgetful," we recommend that you come alongside them with whatever strengths you have for structuring things and help them think through what needs to be done and by when.

Admittedly, that can be easier said than done. They'll never change who they are, and you'll never change them, either. When you point out that the way to tackle the big project due at the end of the semester is to do a little bit this week and a little bit next week and a little bit the following week and so on, you're liable to get a response of, "Yeah, you're right. But this week I have to concentrate on my recital, so I'll worry about that next week."

All we're saying is, do what you can. Even just seeing a suggested plan for how they might accomplish what they need to accomplish in school can be helpful. For one thing, it takes a bunch of vague "stuff" that hangs over them and breaks it down into bite-size, doable pieces.

This is another example of where having a working relationship with your child's teacher can pay off. By communicating with the teacher and asking them for strategies or backup, you may get great input from them that ends up solving your problem very effectively.

# 12

# the
# laboratory
# of life

n this chapter we want to mention specific ways to make giftedness observations as your child works their way through school. Schools are about much more than reading, writing, and 'rithmetic. They also serve as a kind of laboratory for life, a somewhat controlled environment outside the home where you can observe how your child's giftedness expresses itself in interactions with the wider world.

## Observe How Your Child Relates to Other Students

Do you remember the playground scene we looked at in chapter 4? Some children were playing in a group. Others were playing in pairs. Others were by themselves. Each child's interactions were driven by their particular giftedness.

The same basic dynamic can be seen in a typical classroom at a school. Only now the children express their giftedness in more developed ways. And things are also starting to get more complicated as the children receive feedback from their peers and teachers in terms of how those people are experiencing them.

As a parent, you naturally want your child to have a good experience at school, which likely means you want them to "fit in" and feel a sense of belonging. That's great! But hold that aspiration lightly. It would be a mistake to try and "make" the school setting work for your child. Yes, you can and should be their advocate, as we've described. But you can't engineer around the fact that for your child, as for most children, school is probably the primary venue in which they will begin to discover how they, with their unique giftedness, interact with others in the wider world beyond the family.

**You want them to "fit in" and feel a sense of belonging. That's great! But hold that aspiration lightly.**

If you watch carefully over time, you can learn volumes about what might be called your child's relational style, as well as the styles of other children. Here are just a handful of possibilities that your child might turn out to be:

- *an initiator* who is gregarious and outgoing, always starting conversations and enrolling others in new activities.

- *a competitor*, as we saw in Jenna, always turning things into a contest that they can win.

- *an explainer* who seems to take an interest in other children understanding things.

- *a boss* who instinctively tries to take charge and hand out marching orders.

- *a daredevil* who doesn't seem to mind taking risks and being the first to try things that other children shrink back from.

- *a protector* who speaks up and steps in when another child is getting taken advantage of.

- *a comic* who seems to enjoy getting a response from their classmates by acting goofy or making a face or doing the unexpected.

- *an observer* who sort of sits back and takes it all in and only occasionally shares what's on their mind.

- *a captain* who seems to have a knack for ending up as the leader, often because the other children seem to just expect it.

- *an imaginator* who frequently invites other children into imaginary worlds of play and adventure.

- *an organizer* who tells everybody where they fit into a plan.

- *a standout* who periodically does something that makes a statement and catches everyone's attention.

- *a problem solver* who comes alive when something needs to be fixed or figured out or resolved.

- *The quiet creative*, like Danice (not all creatives are quiet), who interacts very little with the other students, yet speaks eloquently through occasional creative expressions like a poem or song.

- *an encourager* who instinctively seeks out the downcast child, the lonely child, the hurting child, the disappointed child, and comes alongside with solace and support.

- *a participant* who is never so happy as when they are part of a group, doing something together.

Again, these are just a few suggestions. You may not find your child in any of these descriptions. But notice the wide variety of ways in which a child can end up relating to their peers.

However your child chooses to interact with others, trust the expression of their giftedness. In other words, accept who they are and are motivated to be. Some parents have very strong opinions about their child ending up as the "leader." Never mind whether their child has any motivation or strengths for leading others, at least the way the parents recognize "leading." Other parents are determined that their kid has to be the smartest one in the class. Never mind whether their child has any interest in academic pursuits.

All of the styles described above have extraordinary value and purpose, and none is any "better" or "worse" than the others. Your child is who they are. They "be who they be." What schooling allows both them and you to do is gain deeper insight into how their being uniquely inclines toward interacting with others.

And as your child grows older, you can help them gain that insight by talking with them about their interactions with the other kids. School gives them an experience of how others who are not their family perceive them. We might call those perceptions the "natural consequences of being who they are." For example, the child who likes to be in charge will likely find that others sometimes push back when they attempt to take control. The child who likes to show what they can do may find that classmates get tired of being their audience. Likewise, a child may find that other children are drawn to them or consistently choose them for a team activity, or that others tend to follow their lead. For many children, school is the first time they experience peers responding to who they naturally are.

## Observe How Your Child Responds to Authority

In addition to placing your child in proximity to more children, school also places certain demands and expectations on them. They are no longer autonomously free to choose what they will do and how they will do it. That means your child is experiencing some of their first encounters with authority beyond your own authority as their parent. Obviously, the teachers will be the main authority figures in that setting.

As always, your child's giftedness will factor heavily into how they regard authority and how they respond to it. We can use some of the descriptors listed above to illustrate:

- *a child who tends to initiate* may be quick to figure out what the teacher wants and then start recruiting everyone else into that objective.

- *a child who tends to be a boss* may clash with a teacher who is trying to stay in charge. It's not that the student means to be difficult, but there's an inherent contest of wills in play. If the teacher is perceptive, they can use the student's influence to steer things in a positive direction. They can also help the student gain maturity in the exercise of their gift. However, if the teacher resolves to power up so as to dominate the student, things can go very poorly.

- *a child who tends to be the comic* may frequently find themselves looking up into the glare of a teacher who is not amused with their antics or their unprompted comments in class. On the other hand, a perceptive teacher can turn this child's comic displays into moments of relief or a change of pace for the class, and also find places in the curriculum from time to time that allow this child's humor to have a role.

- *a child who tends to be the organizer* may see themselves as the teacher's sergeant-at-arms, getting everyone lined up with the plan. In turn, the teacher might assign such a child projects to work on that help the teacher out.

- *a child who needs to stand out or make a statement by their unorthodox behavior* may run afoul of a teacher from time to time because they steal the attention at an inopportune moment. On the other hand, a seasoned teacher may recognize

the inherent leadership qualities of such a child, for good or
for bad, and find ways to channel those bids for attention into
positive moments of impact.

- *a child who tends to be a participant* will be more than happy
  to go along with whatever the teacher asks. Their primary
  aim, after all, is to play a part in a group activity. But that also
  means they may struggle with being singled out, or whenever they are called upon to perform in front of the class by
  themself.

As you can see, a great deal depends on the interaction between
your child's giftedness and their teacher's giftedness. Some forms of
giftedness are very much about power and control. If that describes
your child, you've no doubt already seen it at home, so just know that
those gifts will express themselves in ever more sophisticated ways as
they enter school. You can be your child's advocate by letting teachers
know who your child is and what your own hopes and concerns are
for their development.

Having done that, you then want to keep the lines of communication open with the teachers. Receive their feedback with an open mind
and trust them to act wisely in responding positively and proactively
to the unique strengths your child exhibits. A child who constantly
tests limits and boundaries is going to be a handful for any adult. But
sometimes a classroom teacher can actually be more effective than a
parent in getting through to such a child because they have a different
relationship with them.

## Sports and Recreation

Earlier we described the learning styles that academic settings tend
to favor: readers, writers, memorizers, conceptualizers, test takers. So
what about those who learn by figuring things out on the fly, practicing,

collaborating on a team, performing against fixed standards, competing, strategizing, getting immediate feedback, and keeping score in real time? For many of those learners, sports and athletic activities are the one bright spot of their day at school. That's where they excel. That's where their gifts match what's required.

At many schools you can feel the students come alive when they head to the locker rooms in the afternoon. There's an energy, an excitement, a renewed enthusiasm. Students who seemed to be sleepwalking all day (or even actually sleeping) can't wait to get their bodies warmed up and into action. You'll hear whoops, cheers, whistles, laughter, and other sounds of engagement. And as the athletes take to the field, the court, the pool, the track, or wherever their sport takes place, activities that once were considered mere play have now become serious business. It's time to give it your all and show up with your best stuff.

## Coaches

One of the key elements in this auxiliary, extracurricular learning environment is the coach, especially the ones who are gifted to the task of coaching youth. For many of the people we've worked with, an athletic coach ended up making all the difference in their life. The coach not only helped them develop as an athlete, but also served as a mentor.

Dennis is such a person. We happen to have worked with quite a few young adults who attended the middle school where Dennis, now retired, both taught and coached soccer. Many of them have spoken eloquently about Dennis's unwavering belief in their worth. They described his way of patiently but persistently searching for the door that eventually opened not just their mind, but their heart.

Recently Dennis was invited to attend a soccer banquet at his old school. A graduating team member specifically requested his presence because he wanted to honor Dennis publicly as "his person," the individual whose influence had proven indispensable to that young man's growth as a human being.

How many other middle school students must Dennis have impacted like that over the years? No one knows for sure, but what we do know is that countless kids showed up in Dennis's classroom or on the soccer field where he was coaching, totally unaware they were about to be transformed by the experience. He became their mentor, "their person," someone who could clearly see the inner light they radiated. Someone who would stop at nothing to become their biggest champion. Someone who would relentlessly seek to help them become, in truth, the person they were born to be. For Dennis, working with junior high kids wasn't a job, it was a calling. It was the practice of soulcraft—not the filling of a pail but the lighting of a fire.

### Team Performance vs. Individual Performance

By its nature, sports emphasize performance—both individual and team. This dynamic gives you as a parent an opportunity to observe the extent to which your child places value on their own performance versus their team's.

Some people are totally focused on their own individual performance. Not surprisingly, they often are drawn toward sports like golf, tennis (singles), track and field events, gymnastics, swimming, and diving. They may be part of a team, meaning they train and practice with other athletes involved in the same sport. And sometimes that team dynamic may influence where a coach positions them in, say, a tournament or a relay race. But the emphasis is on their personal development and the endless quest for their personal best.

Other sports are much more team-oriented, and even though all the players are expected to excel at their individual game, winning or losing is a team win or loss. Obvious examples are football, basketball, baseball, lacrosse, hockey, and soccer.

So which does your child care about more: how well they perform, or how well their team performs? There's no right or wrong answer, of course. But it's helpful for children to discover over time which one tends to feel more satisfying because that satisfaction may have significant implications later on when they enter the work world.

Indeed, it's rather telling that at The Giftedness Center, one of the most frequent kinds of stories we hear about is being on a sports team as a kid. What kids can learn about themselves by playing Little League or Pop Warner Football or youth soccer is often life-changing. It takes the delight of play to a new level.

**In many ways sports provide children with their first introduction to principles that govern the work world they will someday enter.**

In many ways sports provide children with their first introduction to the principles that govern the work world they will someday enter: working together toward a common goal; the importance of getting along with others; doing things that are hard and discovering that by working together, you and your teammates can rise to the challenge; learning perseverance, resilience, and pulling together in the face of adversity, and sometimes even defeat; and most of all, experiencing the satisfaction of seeing a job well done.

The kid whose sole ambition and dedication for as long as he could remember was to win a footrace often grows up to have a sole ambition and dedication for being Salesperson of the Year, year after year. Likewise, the girl who loved playing catcher on her softball team because she could control the game in ways that helped her team win often grows up to be a project manager who controls a production project at her company in ways that help her team bring the project to completion ahead of schedule and under budget. And what about the prima donna high-scorer on the basketball team? Years later you often find them still picking off the choice assignments, behaving flamboyantly, throwing temper tantrums when things don't go their way, yet turning in such a great performance that they're too valuable for the company to let go.

In short, because sports are so visible and so effective at forcing players to show what they're made of, they can be a great venue for observing some of the detail and texture of your child's giftedness.

## Other Extracurricular Activities

Much of what we've just said about sports also applies to activities like piano lessons, band, orchestra, choir, ballet and dance, theater and drama, debate, and so on. They are all excellent opportunities for parents to make observations about their child's strengths, motivations, relational dynamics, learning style, etc.

However, we should mention that when we interview people about their history of meaningful achievement, they sometimes volunteer the fact that while they participated in an extracurricular activity during elementary school, they dropped it as soon as they got into junior high or high school. When we ask why, they'll say that the only reason they stuck it out as long as they did was because their parents "made them."

That raises an important point about extracurricular activities in general, including sports: make sure your child is taking violin lessons or singing in the choir or devoting their Saturdays to an Odyssey of the Mind team because *they* have energy for doing that activity, not because you've decided that would be a great thing for them to do. Or worse, because you did that activity as a child and loved it, and you've been yearning for the day when your son or daughter would follow in your footsteps.

It's a hard call, we admit. In the first place, how does a six-year-old know what they are asking for when they beg you to sign them up for

Suzuki piano lessons? Is it really some precocious awareness that they have a love of music percolating in their soul? Or is it because their friend Olivia has started taking Suzuki, and that sounds like fun?

Moreover, we've suggested earlier that you give your child opportunities to try out different activities and then watch to see what energizes them. So say you've done that and signed your daughter up for dance lessons. She seems to enjoy dance well enough. How long should she stick with it?

There's no hard and fast rule to answer that question, other than to ask: what is my child getting out of this activity? What is holding them to it? It might be an interest in the subject matter itself, whether music or story or drawing or the movement of one's body. It could be competition. Or being part of a group or team. Or seeing their progress as they get better at the activity over time. Or performing in front of others. Or a bond that they feel with the teacher or instructor.

But if the answer is, essentially, nothing—"My child isn't really getting anything out of this"—then you have to ask whether it's worth continuing. It may be time to try something new.

Just make sure that in making that change your child doesn't adversely affect others. Quitting band three weeks before the spring concert leaves the other musicians in the lurch. That's why it's important to have a heart-to-heart conversation with your child up front, and maybe follow-up conversations along the way, to make sure they understand the virtue of keeping their word. If they sign up for a given period of time, they have a responsibility to show up for the duration and fulfill their commitment. And from a practical standpoint, following through on their commitment keeps you as a parent from paying for a lot of things your child doesn't finish.

But with that said, there's no need to regard quitting as a failure, per se, either your child's or your own. "We tried the clarinet and it didn't work. We tried art lessons and they didn't work." A more positive way to assess the situation would be to try and find out *what* "didn't work" about a given activity, and then use it to brainstorm possibilities for what might "work."

For example: "Damien played clarinet for a couple of years when he started in the band. But he lost interest because he rarely got to play any solos. That's when we realized trumpet might be a better fit for him, because trumpets get lots of solos. It took some persuading with the band teacher, but she finally he let Damien switch to trumpet, and he's been practicing his trumpet like we never saw him do with his clarinet."

## The Child with Learning Challenges

In chapter 6 we mentioned children with disabilities. In talking about the implications of giftedness for education, we can't help but revisit that topic.

By now you may have guessed that we view learning as an inherently positive experience for humans. Some might scoff at that assertion, but we can easily prove it by pointing to the thousands of interviews we have conducted with people to discover their giftedness. One of the most prominent takeaways from that research is the vast number of people who have described a learning activity (in many cases, several of them) as being among the most satisfying experiences of their life.

There's something intrinsic to the human condition that takes delight in growth, in development, in acquiring new skills and/or knowledge, in discovering new things. Learning allows one to feel more empowered, more confident, more competent, more, well, human. And any true teacher (meaning someone gifted to the task of actually causing learning to take place) will tell you that delight physically manifests itself in the eyes of a learner when they finally "get" it. The light comes on!

To be sure, the process of learning itself may sometimes be

daunting, challenging, arduous, tedious, or even dangerous. There may be significant temptations to quit. Yet something mysteriously keeps drawing a learner back to the process—unless, of course, the learner comes to the conclusion that they don't have what it takes.

Here's where we get down to reality. We've already said that society's choice to use a mostly academic model of instruction for its educational system works well for students whose learning styles fit that model. But it unintentionally creates difficulties for those whose learning styles are not a good match for academic learning. That's why sports and other extracurricular activities are such a godsend for many students. Without that, they would simply give up.

**Regardless of a child's given realities, every child desires to learn because learning is what humans do.**

How much greater, then, are the learning challenges for students who have learning disabilities or special needs? Or who are partially or totally blind or severely hearing impaired? Or who have a condition like ADHD, dyslexia, or a speech impediment? Or who have limited mobility or are a wheelchair user? Or who live with a mental or psychological challenge like schizophrenia, depression, or anxiety? Or who have a chronic physical challenge to manage like cystic fibrosis, muscular dystrophy, or leukemia?

Our point is this: regardless of a child's given realities, *every* child desires to learn because learning is what humans do. It's how we grow and develop. And when we press into that phenomenon and examine how learning takes place, we discover that every human has their own unique form of giftedness that predisposes them to learn certain things in certain ways.

That may not be readily apparent to others. Unfortunately, we live in a society that doesn't embrace the great diversity of ways in which people learn. As a result, we so often miss out when those who are "challenged" invite us into the singular, celebratory gift of their presence among us. Instead, we choose to measure the performance and characteristics of human beings against standardized norms, which automatically sets us up to focus on deficits. Rather than define a child by who she is—"who she be" through all the unique ways she expresses herself and seeks to communicate and engage with the world—she's defined by the diagnosis of a deficit, and that pronouncement too easily becomes the primary lens through which she is viewed, and the basis for whatever progress is expected.

> **"I wanted to see her in the light of having explored the place between everything is possible and nothing is possible, to find the most beautiful possibility she was capable of."**

By contrast, one mother poignantly described coming to terms with her young daughter's limitations this way: "I wanted to see her in the light of having explored the place between everything is possible and nothing is possible, to find the most beautiful possibility she was capable of. And then I was ready to fight for all that was here."

If your child has learning challenges, you as their parent can make all the difference in the world by functioning as their champion and advocate. Yes, you look squarely at the realities your child lives with. Those are undeniable. But you can serve your child best by persistently and even relentlessly paying attention to their personhood—and with it, their giftedness. So you give yourself to helping your child discover and pay attention to that. And then make sure that everyone else who interacts with your child pays attention to it—most especially their caregivers and teachers at school. You remain locked onto the possibility of this child of yours, and you advocate for the wholeness of who they are, seeing them through God's eyes as the good gift you were given in this world.

### "Show Them Who You Are!"

Queen Mother Ramonda in the superhero film *Black Panther* illustrates the kind of parental champion we're talking about. Ramonda's husband, T'Chaka, ruler over an African country called Wakanda, has died. Now it is time to crown his son, T'Challa, as king. However, another tribe's leader, M'Baku, has challenged T'Challa for the crown, and the two must decide the outcome in ritual combat to the death.

The fight begins, and M'Baku proves to be a formidable warrior. T'Challa lands a few blows here and there, but soon M'Baku has him disarmed and begins to taunt him. "Where is your God, now?!" he screams, laughing. T'Challa rallies, but suddenly M'Baku grips him tightly in a bear hug and stuns him with a crushing headbutt. Derisively M'Baku sneers, "No powers." Headbutt! "No claws." Headbutt! "No special suit, oh! Just a boy, not fit to lead."

T'Challa is limp, broken, and losing consciousness.

Then he hears a voice. It is not the loudest voice among the din of cheers, jeers, screams, and shrieks swirling around him. But it is the voice T'Challa knows better than any other—for it is the voice of his mother, Ramonda, crying out, "Show him who you are!"

That voice and that word awaken something deep inside T'Challa, and in a flash he retaliates with a massive headbutt that knocks M'Baku backward, freeing T'Challa.

But only for an instant. M'Baku thrusts his spear deep into T'Challa's shoulder, and again it looks as if all is lost. T'Challa stares wide-eyed at his wound, in shock.

And then he erupts: "I am Prince T'Challa, son of King T'Chaka!"

With a ferocity his foe never expected, he takes M'Baku down and wrestles him right to the point of finishing him off. But mercifully he stops short with the words, "You have fought with honor, now yield! Your people need you."

By that means T'Challa wins the contest, and with it, the kingdom.

Comic book heroes act out oversized dramas, to be sure. But is your role as a parent really that different from Queen Ramonda's? You can't fight your child's battles for them, nor should you. But as they "fight" to make their way in the world, your job is to keep calling them back to their core personhood: "Show them who you are! Remember who you are! You are *not* your condition. You are you! You have meaning and a purpose and a gift from your Maker. Let *that* be decisive. Let *that* be your strength and your call and the arc of your destiny!"

But what does that actually look like in the real world—especially when you have a child with severe limitations? In the story that follows, Bev tells about a real-life Queen Ramonda whom she knows personally.

# the barbie doll dream house

Frederick Buechner says that "a miracle is when the whole is greater than the sum of its parts. A miracle is when one plus one equals a thousand."[1] By that calculus, ordinary miracles must be passing by us every day. But do we notice?

## the need to be present

One reason why we overlook miracles is that we are overly conditioned to expect them to show up spectacularly, lit up by fireworks and accompanied by fanfare and spectacle that commands our full attention. Meanwhile, we are rarely present to the mystical epiphany continuously being revealed in the everyday holiness of all our moments.

For example, I have often thought how fragile and fleeting our sense of amazement and wonder is around the miracle of birth. Perhaps it is the sleeplessness, all the crying, the endless round of feedings and diapers and laundry—all of that just so quickly flattens the ecstatic high of the day of delivery under a pile of routine and uninspiring repetitiveness.

With a birth must also be born, or reborn, a recognition that ordinary miracles require *presence*—choosing to fully be there with eyes open, receiving every moment like the gift that it is. I think I can hear you yawning from here, no doubt from sheer sleep deprivation.

But seriously, what if we really looked at every Thing in our path and every One we encounter in *expectation* of wonder? How might changing our lens change what we discern?

For me (Bev), so often it is simply a certain slant of light that falls on me to cast a radiance so irresistible that I have to follow it wherever it leads—even when it takes me further out and deeper in than I ever expected to go.

## susie

So it was on the day I encountered the light of Susie, a fellow mom I had met through a young adults group we both attended some years ago. The group was filled to the brim with young couples like ourselves, who were in that childrearing, career-and-community-building part of life. Susie sparkled with an openness and life-affirming spirit that I found captivating. It became immediately apparent that deep faith drove everything she was.

I don't remember when I found out that her three-year-old daughter, named Libby, had been born prematurely at only twenty-five weeks of pregnancy. Her birth weight was 1 pound, 15 ounces. Three days later, Libby's brain suffered an intraventricular hemorrhage. The result was that the first three years of Libby's life required Susie's constant attention to her daughter's substantial and precarious challenges.

I honestly could not imagine how someone faced with that degree of chronic sorrow could so consistently manage to embody the kind of energy and expectancy I witnessed every single time I saw Susie. But I knew I needed to know. So when Susie invited me over one day, I couldn't wait to be with her, and to meet Libby.

Libby was waiting for me when I arrived, propped up in her little seat in the entryway of their home. She was all dolled up with a pink bow in her flaxen hair, and even though she had never met me before, her whole face lit up with delight when she saw me. All I could think was that she looked like a tiny angel, haloed by the most radiant joy imaginable.

I remember feeling so humbled that morning by Susie's unshake-able optimism and peace-filled outlook throughout our conversation about Libby. She possessed such a calm acceptance in spite of great uncertainty regarding Libby's still-fragile health and major concerns about what her future would look like. I asked Susie to help me understand how she could hold onto such a hopeful outlook while facing such a formidable reality.

## signposts of encouragement

That's when she took me back to the beginning of this journey she was on, in which everything was uncertain and she was forced to struggle with a constant barrage of pressures—pressures that not only affected her child, but also the whole family. She told me that every time she would come to the end of her own resources, she would receive the most incredible word-picture, a visual image in story form that would be exactly what she needed to encourage her heart and mind.

Over time, Susie had collected all the stories she had been given over the years—150 in all! That means 150 hand-drawn sign-posts of encouragement and insight that she believed were heaven-sent to inspire her to live with expectancy, even while traveling that long, unfamiliar path with Libby.

Susie loved sharing those points of light with me. Just listening to her tell the stories of how those word-pictures had come to her was nothing less than transformative. It was like taking a master class in miracles.

# barbie doll dream house

One story she told me in particular I will carry in my heart forever, and it goes like this:

All my life I had wanted a Barbie Doll Dream House. All my friends were getting them, and I could not wait for Christmas to come, believing with all my heart that this would be the year. Then, a week before Christmas, I found a large box under the tree, beautifully wrapped, and I thought to myself, "Aha, it *must* be my Barbie Doll Dream House!"

It was as if I could see it all coming to life in my mind. I spent hours daydreaming, creating elaborate scenes in my imagination that had me playing with my Barbies and arranging their things in their new dream house.

When Christmas morning finally arrived, I ran downstairs and tore into the box with great expectation. But it was not my Dream House after all! Instead, it was some kind of long, flat, black case. And when I opened it up, there were all these pieces inside that looked broken apart, along with a thick manual that had the words, Reflecting Telescope, on the front.

I could feel the tears gathering in my eyes. I had wanted the Dream House with all my heart. I had watched my friends play with their Dream Houses, and I had already started planning in my mind how everything would go in my Dream House, and how much I would love it. I didn't want a telescope. I didn't even know how to put it together. I certainly didn't know what possible use I would have for it.

Just then my father came in. I cried out, "Oh, Father, all my life I've asked you for a Barbie Doll Dream House! Why did you give me a telescope instead?"

He gently gathered me in his arms and said, "So you could see Me more clearly."

I had tears in my own eyes as I listened to her words. I couldn't help but recognize that the Barbie Doll Dream House was a wish made out of plastic, a gift that wouldn't last. Receiving Libby as the telescope God had chosen for her was a lifetime gift, one that Susie would keep learning how to appreciate and understand, trusting that Libby had been made, exactly as she was, to point Susie to undiscovered wonder and be an instrument of grace in this world to reveal more heavenly truth than we could know on our own.

Like the telescope in the story, Susie came to believe that Libby had been given to her just as she was, as a good gift, a special gift. She came to the conviction that through Libby, God would point Susie toward her deepest joy and hope, even though it was found in a place where Susie would have never chosen to go.

Susie and her family moved to Chicago not long after telling me that story, and today Libby is thirty-four. She is still the beam of light she was when I first met her at age three. In spite of being unable to walk or talk, and still 100 percent dependent on her parents, with whom she lives, Libby's life has been, in Susie's words, the most profound story of rescue and redemption imaginable. The grace that has covered her each and every one of her days has been undeniable.

Libby has undergone seventy-nine surgeries in her life, including one six-month hospitalization that involved multiple shunt revisions and life-threatening brain infections. Susie told me one of Libby's neurosurgeons said he had seen miraculous things happen in her brain while he operated on her that he knew he had not done.

Libby's cognitive ability to understand everything around her remains remarkable. She has persistently worked to achieve the highest educational standing she could, and eventually she completed her high school degree. She also took great delight in serving as a bridesmaid in her brother's wedding.

Not long ago, Susie sent me an updated photo of Libby, and what a beautiful gift it was! To see this sweet child whose future was so precarious, now all grown up and thriving at thirty-four years of age, was overwhelming. Surely her story could only be a tribute to Susie's story of relentlessly championing the most beautiful possibility for her daughter while embracing the wholeness of her personhood just as she is. Libby was as exquisitely dressed and cared for as on that day I had first met her, and even though many years had passed, I would have known her anywhere by the signature joy I recognized on her face.

I immediately phoned Susie, and we indulged in a long-overdue conversation to catch up. From time to time, I could hear Libby vocalizing in the background. Susie explained that Libby knew we were talking about her story, and that was her way of saying "Amen," lifting her voice to add her own praise in response to our conversation about God's constant care throughout her life.

Susie believes with all her heart—and how could I not see it for myself?—that Libby is that "good and perfect gift" that only comes from above.[2] All she is made to be points to the wonder, the miracles that are daily possible all around us. Her reflection of joy shines each day, as the telescope she is, that every moment of every life is sacred.

# PART IV

# the teenage years

# 13

## the essence of adolescence

Western civilization has made countless advances in bettering the human condition, but helping adolescents navigate puberty with confidence has not been among them. Whereas many cultures have well-established rites and rituals to usher young people into adulthood, the West offers preteens few, if any, signs or symbols to mark the day when they are finally considered adults and should consider themselves adults, as well.

Perhaps this is why adolescence as a season of life is starting sooner and lasting longer in developed societies. And perhaps also why the term *adolescence* has such negative connotations for many. One psychologist reports that for many parents of adolescents, "the common fear statement sounds like this: 'Parenting is much more scary now than it was for my parents when I was growing up, or for my grandparents raising my parents. There are so many more hazards for teenagers today than there were back then!'"[1]

Adolescence can be a precarious season, for sure. And your feelings about parenting your child through it will likely mirror the feelings *you* experienced at that season of your life. What do you remember most about your adolescent years? What were the highlights?

What were the hardest parts? What were the emotions that most dominated your soul?

As you ponder those questions, can you start to see some connections between your own giftedness and what happened back there? (We hope that as you've been paying attention to your child's giftedness, you've started paying attention to your own, too.)

In this section we want to look at adolescence through the lens of giftedness in hopes of shedding insight both on your own past and on your present task of helping your child grow into a healthy adult.

## What Changes and What Doesn't?

The most uncontested fact of adolescence is that one's body undergoes profound changes. "Growing up" means growth spurts of height, weight, and overall bodily composition as bones harden and muscles grow. The brain eliminates unneeded neural pathways in a massive effort to operate more efficiently, as well as more abstractly. Everything is awash in hormones, which act as the engineers of what amounts to a giant expansion project. Their efforts are largely organized around puberty and preparing the body for sexual reproduction. That means a lot of new physical experiences for a child, which in turn means a lot of strange and unexpected feelings—some good, some not so good, many just downright confusing.

It goes without saying that one of the best things you can do as a parent is to prepare your child for these changes long before they ever happen.

Your child's physical changes also mean changes in just about every other area of their life. They begin to realize they have powers they hadn't noticed. People they've ignored for years suddenly start to look interesting and even attractive. New friends appear. New interests start popping up. Behaviors and habits that had seemed set in stone only months before suddenly get left behind. Emotions once expressed in fits and spurts now settle into longer-lasting moods.

To a parent, these changes can range from seeming curious to humorous to cute to annoying to perplexing to troubling to unacceptable. (Note that your child may experience them similarly.) For many, the fact that "my little boy/girl is growing up" can be quite unsettling.

But here's one thing you can hold onto: despite all the changes taking place physically, emotionally, psychologically, and socially for your child, one thing that doesn't fundamentally change is their giftedness. That core remains what it always has been. Don't lose sight of that!

We stress this because adolescence itself can be stressful to parents, not just their child. After all, what do you do when your thirteen-year-old daughter ends yet another knock-down-drag-out argument over the stupidest thing by stomping off, screaming, "You're a terrible mother! You're the worst mother in the world! Why did I ever have to be born into this family?" At such a moment you can feel like an utter failure. Like you've done everything wrong, and as a result, you're certain that you've "lost" your child.

You haven't lost anything! That bratty tween who just told you the nastiest thing she could have possibly said is the same person you cuddled in your arms thirteen years before as a newborn. Your task now is the same as it was then—to steward that infant person you were given into an adult person according to The Way of Your Child. That child and her Way are now slogging through the challenges of adolescence, and it's a messy journey to be sure. A lot can threaten to get everyone off course. But don't lose sight of your child's personhood. Even in her impudence and insolence, what is she expressing about herself—her *self*? Look past the insult, if you can, to see the person you are seeking to guide toward maturity.

And also stay grounded and secure in

**When there's tumult with your child, it can be quite tempting to start doubting yourself and your handling of things.**

your own giftedness. That, too, never fundamentally changes. But when there's tumult with your child, it can be quite tempting to start doubting yourself and your handling of things. Because of how they're wired, many parents require a positive response from others in order to know that they've succeeded. So if they don't get any response from their sulking tween, or worse, a negative response, they can quickly begin to take everything personally and start sinking in emotional quicksand. That same "response" dynamic that made them the hero in their child's younger years now sets them up to be wounded by their child's sullen attitude or unkind comments.

## The Neutrality of Giftedness

Whatever else happens during adolescence, it's when young people start realizing there are some real differences between boys and girls. That leads to a question we are often asked: Is giftedness different for boys than it is for girls? Or another version: Do boys tend to have certain kinds of giftedness and girls other kinds of giftedness?

The short answer is no. Giftedness turns out to be gender-neutral. That is, there is no such thing as "male strengths" as opposed to "female strengths." The power and diversity of giftedness appears to be distributed across men and women alike.

We say that on the basis of having studied thousands of people's patterns of giftedness over several decades. If the name is removed from a description of one's giftedness, it's impossible to tell whether the person in question is a man or a woman. For that matter, it's impossible to tell whether the individual is young or old, or what their race or ethnicity is, or their socioeconomic status, or any of the other characteristics that people today so often claim as their "identity."

Giftedness is the most neutral—and also the most direct—way that we are aware of to access and see the personhood of an individual. That's why we always feel we are walking on holy ground whenever we have the privilege of helping someone discover their giftedness. We're being invited into the very heart of who that person is. Of "who they be."

Of course, the neutrality of giftedness in terms of gender can prove disruptive to various social constructs and cultural norms. For instance, we've occasionally worked with a male entrepreneur who has built an extremely prosperous business and now wants to identify a successor, preferably from his family. Let's say he has three sons and one daughter. An analysis of the three sons' giftedness bears out what they've already told us: none of them has the slightest interest in taking over their father's business. Meanwhile, the daughter has a lifelong history of leading, analyzing, decision-making, selling, convincing, bargaining, and working to get results through others—all of which would make her a perfect fit as her father's successor. So we present that finding to the patriarch, and he pushes back, saying, "But she's a girl!"

It was a new thought for that man when we pointed out that success in running a business is not a matter of gender but of having the right stuff to run that business.

Are there differences between boys and girls? There are obvious physical differences, but beyond that we leave it to other experts to weigh in on that question. In this book our primary concern is your child, and the primary difference that matters for them is not the number of X- or Y-chromosomes they have, but the uniqueness of their gift—and how it fits them to make a singularly valuable contribution to the world.

# 14

# peer groups: mixing but not melting

E arlier we told the story of Bill baking an angel food cake when he was five. That impulse to periodically cook up something random continues to this day. So not long ago, while we were in the thick of putting this book together, Bill had the idea of taking a break to bake a batch of chocolate chip cookies. Not from store-bought dough, mind you, but (as with the angel food cake) totally from scratch and in search of the ultimate chocolate chip cookie.

Having found the perfect recipe, he commenced to sift together the flours, the baking soda, the salt. In a mixer he creamed the butter and sugars together until just right. He added the eggs, stirred in the vanilla, then mixed in the dry ingredients.

At that point the recipe instructed, "Reduce speed to low and drop chocolate pieces in, incorporating them without breaking them."

Isn't that exactly what needs to happen in junior high and high schools today—incorporate the kids without breaking them?

Think about it. Schools mix together a lot of different ingredients.

But just as the key ingredient in a chocolate chip cookie are the chocolate chips, so the key ingredient in a school are the students. Yet how much care is taken to incorporate the kids without breaking them?

We're talking here about social interactions and fitting in. As a parent, you want your adolescent to fit in at school and feel a sense of belonging among their peers. Yet at the same time, you want them to avoid peer pressure—to maintain their individuality, and also to resist any negative influences that might come their way.

Being a part of the group—while still being oneself. Can you see the tension between those two? You want your child to incorporate, but not break. To mix but not melt. You want to end up with chocolate chip cookies, after all, not brownies.

Fortunately, your child's giftedness can help you (and them) with that.

## A Fix for the Cliques

As we pointed out in the previous chapter, middle school children start experiencing all kinds of strange things as puberty sets in. It can be pretty scary. The natural reaction to such anxiety is to work very hard at not "sticking out" or looking odd. A herd mentality then takes hold. Everyone starts wearing the same clothes, liking the same music, using the same language, signing up for the same social media. The ideal is to be "liked" and to "belong," with the ultimate prize to be "popular." The worst that can happen to a kid at that age is to be excluded as "weird" or "strange."

There are powerful dynamics at play here. On the one hand, it's very human to want to belong and feel included. In addition, many forms of giftedness are all about being part of a team and contributing to a group effort. And other forms instinctively seek to include other people in a group activity.

That's all good. But when the desire to belong is driven more by a fear of being excluded or left behind, that's not good. And when a child starts to repress parts of themselves so as to "fit in," that's even worse, especially if it means repressing—rather than expressing—their giftedness.

Add to this mix the reality that certain kids end up becoming the "popular" ones. **For many students, school seems like a dangerous place.** Maybe it's their charm, their swagger, their "coolness," or whatever. But something about them causes other kids to start following them and taking their cues from them. (We would argue that this is actually a function of the popular kids' giftedness—often, however, turned to its "dark side," meaning they use their gifts in selfish or hurtful ways.)

Packs of adolescents arranged in concentric rings of inclusivity/exclusivity based on popularity can quickly become a toxic social network of cliques. Which is exactly what we find in countless schools today. For many students, school is not at all a socially inviting place. Just the opposite: school seems like a dangerous place, which only adds to the angst they are already experiencing as adolescents. Add social media to that toxic brew, and life can seem downright cruel and cutthroat.

So how do you parent your child through such a system, especially if they are not one of the "popular" kids? Well, one of your trump cards, as always, is your child's giftedness.

Here's how that works. Adolescence is exactly the point in life when a child's giftedness begins to express itself in more sophisticated ways that will ultimately become adult ways. You want to encourage your child to lean into their strength, their uniqueness, not hide it away in order to "fit in" with their peers.

### Rocket Man: Hank

Consider Hank as an example. When Hank was little, he took apart almost any gadget he could find: clocks, radios, discarded CD players, fans, computers—anything that no longer worked. He had a fascination in trying to figure out how things "work."

That led to putting together motorized models during his elementary school years. Some were kits that he bought and assembled, but most were contraptions he glued and bolted together out of old LEGO blocks, balsa wood, wire, and a big box of electronic odds and ends he had labeled "Parts." His fascination had grown beyond just discovering how things worked, to how to make them work "better" and "faster."

Then Hank turned twelve. One of his buddies got a model rocket for his birthday. Hank had read about model rockets, but now he had a chance to see one up close. The experience hooked him instantly, and he begged his parents to buy him a starter kit of his own.

Hank's parents, to their credit, gave the request some thought. Would model rockets be a good fit for their son? They knew he had always loved to take things apart and put things together. They also knew he had spent hours and hours perfecting motorized model cars and such. Building rockets seemed like taking things to a whole new level. But then, wasn't that the point, to keep developing one's skills and competencies in accordance with one's bent? So they bought him the starter kit.

Hank applied the same energy and focus to building rockets that he had had in building model cars. In short order, he was buying the most complicated kits, then designing and assembling models of his own. By the time he got to high school, he had a fairly advanced knowledge of rocketry (for a teenager).

Largely based on that experience, Hank applied and was accepted to the engineering school of a state university. In the second semester of his sophomore year, his class took a field trip one Saturday to a rocket range where, under the supervision of the Air Force, they launched a 9-foot rocket they had designed and built as a team. The next year they went back to the same site to see if they could launch a

150-pound rocket to a height of 60,000 feet and successfully return it to earth undamaged.

Now what matters for our discussion here is that Hank's interest in rocketry during his teen years made him somewhat immune to the peer pressures of school. Sure, he knew that some kids called him a "nerd" and a "geek." Others just ignored him as "the guy who has that strange hobby," while others just accepted that rocketry was his "thing." The point is, he wasn't looking to his peers to validate who he was. He had his own sense of self and his own, unique way of expressing that self.

Hank was hardly a popular kid at school. But then, he didn't really care about that. He was friendly enough, but he shied away from the cliques. In time, he found his friends, his "tribe," as it were, in a handful of other students whose giftedness also inclined toward mechanical systems, how stuff works, building "cool" contraptions, and (as is true for so many juvenile boys) pyrotechnics.

Like Hank's parents, you have a huge opportunity as your child comes into adolescence and their developing strengths start coming into their own. That's the very time you want to give them every bit of encouragement and aid them in every way you can to own their gift and gain experience in expressing it.

## But Sometimes It Takes a Village

Hank knew what he wanted, and his parents were supportive. But some teenagers seem to resist any overt suggestions from their parents. That's where it pays for you as a parent to be proactive about solidly connecting your family to a larger extended family and/or community, if possible. Getting actively involved in a church or other faith community, sports team, extracurricular activity group at school, neighborhood association, workout facility, and other opportunities ups the odds that your son or daughter will run into other like-minded peers or adults who could make a significant difference during this critical time in their life. Adolescents need peers who have similar interests, as well as other adults besides their parents in their life. You cannot be your son or daughter's only source of support.

## Relating to Teams

We've pointed out the pitfalls of cliques, but adolescence also presents your teen with opportunities to be involved in legitimate team and group activities. Sports teams are an obvious example, as are bands, orchestras, choirs, and the like. But there are also group projects in classes, student government roles, a variety of clubs and interest groups, service projects, and plenty of informal group-oriented gatherings.

All of these venues give you an opportunity to make closer observations about how your child relates to teams. And now that your child is getting older, you can invite them to offer their own observations and comments about how they experience group activities. For example:

- What team or group does your child especially thrive in? What is satisfying to them about being part of that group? How would they describe their role within the group?

- What team or group has been disappointing for your child? Can your child point to anything specific that caused that disappointment? Can you identify anything that was missing from that team that could have made the experience better?

- Can you identify any conditions that are critical in order for a group activity to "work" for your teen? For example: "There must be order and structure." "There must be a strong leader." "There must be a well-defined goal." "There must be fairness, honesty, and other values that my child feels strongly about." "There must be praise and affirmation for a job well done."

- Over time, as you step back and look at your child's history of working with various teams and groups, what general observations can you make about how they engage with teams? What has been the best team experience your child ever had? What made that experience so positive (in *their* opinion)? What was satisfying to your child about that experience?

- Do you have a child who generally prefers to work independently rather than on a team? If so, what do they see as the benefits of doing things on their own rather than with others? Are there any special conditions in which your child does like to collaborate with others?

How your child experiences teams and groups at this age is something of an indicator for how they'll interact with teams and groups as an adult in the work world. Despite the fact that American culture has traditionally tended to celebrate the achievements of individuals, the reality is that virtually everything of consequence in our world is accomplished by groups and teams of people working together. So it's important for your child to become aware of how they most naturally relate to others in a larger organizational context, and how they can make their best contribution to that effort.

## But Then, Some People Are Individualists

The crazy thing about giftedness is that as soon as you say that groups and teams do most of the world's work, you're confronted with the question: So what about the people who don't want to be on a team?

Keisha is such a person. Keisha is what we call an individualist. She has nothing against teams, but when it comes to her own tasks, Keisha generally wants to take sole responsibility for what's on her plate and mostly work on her own to get things done. If she needs anyone else's input, she'll ask for it. Otherwise, leave her be.

Again, most people need a group or team, but we certainly see plenty of individualists like Keisha in our work. Perhaps you have a son or daughter like that, who instinctively tends to choose their own company and is quite comfortable just doing their own thing. Hank, whom we met earlier, is such an individualist.

If you have an individualist for a child, think of them as a soloist who makes music on their own for much of the piece and then occasionally joins the larger chorale in a rousing chorus. Many artists, novelists, salespeople, researchers, surgeons, designers, software engineers, chefs, psychologists, lawyers, jewelers, and field goal kickers are wired that way.

But as with all forms of giftedness, there can be a dark side to being an individualist (there can also be a dark side to being a team person). If an individualist is not careful, they can easily become isolated. What's the difference?

An isolated person is not simply on their own. They're cut off from people, and sometimes even from the environmental factors that support their giftedness. Think of it as trying to survive without air, water, and food. Some teens—by virtue of their independent ways—can drift into isolation. They may stay holed up in their room for hours, even days. Their parents may take the attitude, "This is just how teenagers are," and leave them alone.

But that's not helpful—or healthy—for your child. Even if their giftedness predisposes them to prefer doing activities on their own, their gift is given in order to make a contribution to others. They need to let their gift *drive* them toward something outside of themself.

Adolescence is a tough season to navigate, even with the best of support from family and friends. And while teenagers vary as to their sociability, make sure your individualist adolescent is getting the "air, water, and food" their soul needs during this growth season through healthy communication and plenty of involvement with family and community.

# 15

# the priceless presence of models and mentors

Jada was a child who seemed to have no giftedness—at least, none that her parents could identify. She was an average student but seemed bored most of the time, listless. She was like a spectator watching the world go by.

Until her ninth-grade history class. That's when she encountered Mr. Jackson. Frederick Octavius Jackson was a short man with an imposing presence. His great-great-great-grandfather had been born an enslaved person, freed by the Emancipation Proclamation, then forced to become a sharecropper in Mississippi.

## Mr. Jackson

Frederick was the first in his family to receive a college education. He majored in history and graduated third in his class. He went on to complete his master's degree and then earned his PhD in American history, writing his dissertation on the 761st Tank Battalion, the first predominantly African-American tank battalion to serve in World

War II. His grandfather had fought in the 761st and often told him stories of their exploits under General Patton and what happened at The Battle of the Bulge.

Mr. Jackson brought all of that and more each day to his ninth-grade history class, which he invariably taught in a three-piece suit and bow tie. Without being asked, his students responded to him with "Yes, sir," and "No, sir." He was stern but kind, a man who chose his words carefully. And his students hung on every word. He didn't "teach" so much as he told stories. He not only brought history to life in the vivid characters he created for his class, he invited the students who sat transfixed by those portrayals into that history. He was the only teacher in the school ever known to have brought the quarterback of the football team to tears during one of his presentations.

**She felt safe because somehow she could tell that Mr. Jackson cared.**

So when Mr. Jackson assigned Jada's class a research project and told them, "Now if any of you ladies or gentlemen need assistance coming up with a topic, please make an appointment with me, and we can discuss it," Jada was the first to sign up to see him. Indeed, she couldn't wait to see him. Some of her friends were intimidated by Mr. Jackson, but Jada felt absolutely no fear as she opened the door to his classroom for her appointment. If anything, she felt safe because somehow she could tell that Mr. Jackson cared.

As soon as she entered, Mr. Jackson stood up. "Miss Waters," he said, nodding to her. "So good to see you." He invited her to sit in a chair to the side of his desk. As soon as she was seated, he sat down, breathed deeply, and placed his hands flat on his desk. Then he looked her in the eye and asked, "How may I help you this afternoon, young lady?"

"Thank you, sir. You assigned us the research project today, and you said that if we needed help selecting a topic, we should see you. So that's why I'm here."

"I see," he replied as if honored that she would take him up on his offer. Then he looked at her—although not really at her, but more like inside her. It was as if he was trying to set her in context and divine the paths, the choices, the accidents, and the providence that had brought her to this moment. Finally he said, "Tell me, where did your people come from?"

"My people, sir?" She was confused. "You mean, my parents?"

Mr. Jackson chuckled lightly and replied, "Of course, your parents. But I mean your forebears, your ancestors, your heritage. You've heard me talk about my great-great-great-grandfather and the others who came before me. What can you tell me about those who came before you?"

Jada looked back at him with a blank stare. She didn't know how to even begin to answer his question. "I'm not really sure, sir. I mean, my mom says she has Jamaican roots." She knew nothing about her father's background.

"I see," he replied, although Jada remained uncertain as to what, exactly, he was "seeing." Finally, he sat back in his chair, clasped his hands together and dropped them in his lap. "Well, then, I believe you've identified your topic," he said matter-of-factly, as if the issue was settled.

Jada sat for a moment, visibly perplexed. "I'm not sure I see what you mean, sir. What is my topic?"

## "You have much to learn, but also much to offer"

Mr. Jackson looked off as if he were standing in front of a packed theater, his deep voice booming out, "A people without the knowledge of their past history, origin, and culture is like a tree without roots!" He let the final "s" linger and die out. Then he looked at his young pupil. "Do you know who said that?"

"No, sir."

He snorted and said, "Why, that's Marcus Garvey. Do you know who he was?"

Jada shook her head.

"You should. He was a Jamaican. One of the most famous of Jamaicans. He had a vision to unite all the Black peoples of the world and establish a Black nation in Africa. My great-grandfather was a porter for the railroads in his early twenties, and during a trip to New York City he heard Marcus Garvey make a speech in Harlem. My grandfather told me that his father had never heard a man who could inspire others with such hope and belief in a better future."

Mr. Jackson mused for an instant, then continued. "Actually, Garvey got that quote from the Professor. I'm talking about Charles Seifert, of course. His father was the African overseer of a plantation in Barbados, and he had a set of books about Africa that were written long before slavery. Charles taught himself history by reading those books. That's why they called him the Professor. While Marcus Garvey was in Harlem, he lived in Seifert's home, and that's where he picked up that quote. Professor Seifert used to say it all the time."[1]

Having recounted this narrative to Jada, Mr. Jackson summed everything up by declaring, "You have much to learn."

This time Jada recognized what her teacher was driving at. "So you're saying I should make Jamaica my topic?"

"No, Miss Waters, not Jamaica, but the Jamaica that is in you. The Jamaica that gave you life. That gave you your people, your heritage, your birthright. History is not a set of facts. It is a living story of which you are a part. Find out where you fit in that story. Discover your place so as to know your roots and where you stand. Then you can add your part to the story and do so with integrity and honor."

Jada wasn't sure how she knew it, but she knew the conference was over. "Thank you, Mr. Jackson," she said, standing up. "You've been very helpful."

Mr. Jackson stood up as well, and walked her to the door. Opening it in his gentlemanly way, he sent her off with the words, "You have much to learn, Miss Waters, but never forget that you also have much to offer. I can't wait to see what you discover."

## An Inflection Point

That appointment with Mr. Jackson proved to be an inflection point in Jada's education. With what can only be described as ferocity, she threw herself into researching everything she could find about Jamaica. For the next four weeks her parents hardly saw her, she spent so much time online reading articles and websites, and at the library poring over books, encyclopedias, and atlases. She pulled together a thirty-page paper to hand in, for which she received an A-, the highest grade she had ever gotten on anything in school to that point.

The next year she signed up for an elective in Mr. Jackson's course on European history post–World War II, in which she finished with an A. Interestingly, the grades in her other courses started trending up, as well. By her senior year she was making mostly As and Bs, with an occasional C+ in math and science subjects. But it was clear she loved history. Not history, really, but the stories of what happened in times past.

When it came time to apply for college, Jada asked Mr. Jackson for recommendations. He suggested that she seemed to have a particular knack for political history, and that he knew people in that field at Yale, The University of Chicago, and Vanderbilt. Jada's parents gasped when she told them she was planning to apply to those schools, as they would be far too expensive. But thanks to Mr. Jackson's letters of recommendation and the scholarships that Jada's parents had known nothing about until she applied and was accepted, Jada graduated in the upper 10 percent of her class and enrolled at Vanderbilt, where she excelled as a history major, focusing on political history.

## Transforming Impact

Every parent who believes in prayer should get down on their knees every night and pray that a Mr. Jackson comes into their child's life.

And then they should actively be on the lookout for the countless Mr. Jacksons who are out there, hidden in plain sight.

We're talking about individuals who, for reasons no one totally understands, make a transformational impact on a young person's life and destiny. That person could be a teacher, like Mr. Jackson, or an athletic coach like Dennis, whom we met in chapter 12, or a trainer, or a theater director, or a piano instructor, or a youth group leader, or a manager at a part-time job. They can have almost any role in terms of their day job, but their value to your child is the profound influence they have in helping your child focus on what matters and gaining direction and greater self-confidence.

**Every parent who believes in prayer should get down on their knees every night and pray that a Mr. Jackson comes into their child's life.**

In popular terms, we call these people models or mentors (although in truth, your child will probably never use those terms; they will just refer to that person as "Mr. Jackson," or whomever). In our work, these modeling figures show up regularly in the giftedness stories people tell us. In fact, we estimate that a model or mentor is a key element in the motivational patterns of 75 percent to 85 percent of people.

Think about that! We're suggesting that *for at least three out of four people in this world, having a model or mentor-type figure in their life is not simply a "nice" thing to have; it is vital to their functioning!* Without such a person, three out of four people will languish, motivationally speaking.

If we're right about that, then two things need to happen. One is that younger people need to be proactive in seeking out models and mentors. The other is that older people need to be proactive in serving as models and mentors.

No one can force such a relationship. There's a chemistry that has to be there, and as we say, it's kind of a mystery as to how that happens. Why should a fifty-seven-year-old male PhD in history have any appeal to a fourteen-year-old female ninth grader who up to that point has had zero interest in school, let alone history? But there it is. Go figure!

But also, go pray!

# 16

# self-discipline

Kyle's parents are arguing about yet another terrible report card he has brought home from school. His mother is near tears as she tries to calm down her husband, who is furious. "Honey, he's doing the best he can. But between basketball and his job and all the homework they load on him at school, he's just overwhelmed half the time."

"Overwhelmed? Are you kidding me? He spends most of the time in his room goofing off and texting his friends. If he keeps that up, he's going to go nowhere."

"Maybe we should get him a tutor," Kyle's mother suggests.

"No way I'm paying for a tutor. That would just be throwing good money away." Then Kyle's father pronounces his summary take on the root of the problem: "All that boy needs is some self-discipline!"

## Identifying the "Self" in Self-Discipline

Self-discipline. Maybe your parents told you to go find some as you struggled your way through school. Or maybe you're now the parent telling your teenager he needs more of it. But there's a whole school of thought that says the key to doing well in school and in life is to forsake the easy path and the distractions of leisure and pleasure in order to concentrate on hard work and productivity. It's very much in line with the Protestant work ethic, and you can hear it in the oft-repeated popular slogan "no pain, no gain."

It's hard to argue with that philosophy. If you want to build muscle, you've got to exercise. If you want to reap a harvest, you've got to till the soil and plant the crops. If you want to save money for your retirement, you have to put money into savings instead of spending it frivolously. If you want an A on the exam, you have to study the material to be covered on the exam until you know it well enough to earn an A.

Sounds simple enough. And yet it's not quite enough, because it overlooks the role of *motivation* in one's efforts and achievements. The self-discipline school of thought says that self-discipline is simply a matter of the will: you make up your mind and you do it. Okay, but what does it mean to "make up your mind"? It's more than a choice. Something drives that choice, and that something is called *motivation*, which is a kind of desire.

Remember what we said earlier in the book about intrinsic motivation that comes from within, as opposed to extrinsic motivation that comes from the outside? If the motivation to do something is coming from the outside—that is, from someone else—then what's driving the behavior is not really *self*-discipline, it's "*someone else's*-discipline."

To use the example above: Kyle may decide (or to use his dad's term, "make up his mind") to sit down and open up his textbooks and study because his dad has threatened to ground him if he doesn't make better grades. And that may in fact "work." In turn, his dad may celebrate that behavior by telling the boy's mother, "See, once he applied himself and got some self-discipline, he pulled his grades up." But all that's really happened is that Kyle has been coerced into meeting his father's expectations regarding his grades.

## Where There's a Will, There's Also the Way of the Child

For some parents, that's all that matters, and that may be because they've never known any other way. They were coerced into performing by their parents, just as their parents were by their parents, and so on. Meanwhile, in the work world, many employers still believe that their workers have to be coerced to do the work, so they use various forms of external motivation to keep them on task.

**Coerced effort never turns into lasting effort.**

But coerced effort never turns into lasting effort, nor will it ever be someone's best effort. Kyle may do just enough studying to avoid being grounded. But then what? He'll likely go right back to his old ways over the next six-week period, resulting in another bad report card. Will his father then threaten more punishment in order to ensure that his son finds some "self-discipline"? That hardly seems like a workable setup for either Kyle or his parents.

Because it's not. Humans were never intended to be slaves or prisoners, forced to do the bidding of someone else. Each person has been endowed with a core motivational drive that compels them to act. Again, that intrinsic motivation is a kind of desire: a person *wants* to do their "motivational thing," whatever it is. As a result, discipline is never really a problem when a person is acting from their core drive. In that sense, self-discipline genuinely is *self*-discipline. The person does what they must do in order to satisfy that core motivational drive.

Intrinsic motivation in no way eliminates the need for "hard work" to get results. But notice: it supplies the satisfaction that makes the "hard" aspect of the work worth going through. That's why the problem-solver, driven to get the correct answer, stays at the task until they've got the correct answer. It's why the reporter, driven to "get the story," pursues the story day and night until they've tracked it down. It's why the influencer, driven to make a certain number of sales, keeps

**We never say that people should just do what they "like" to do. But doing what you're born to do—that's another matter.**

dialing new leads until they've hit their quota. It's why our father, who was driven to say things people could never forget, lay awake at night wordsmithing phrases, crafting illustrations, and working out the pacing of his delivery so as to become indelibly memorable to his students the next day.

We never say that people should just do what they "like" to do. That would turn them into entitled narcissists, and we certainly don't need more of those! But doing what you're *born* to do, what you're designed to do—that's another matter. We're all for self-discipline, but if that's going to be the standard, let's make sure we're asking our children to act from *self*-discipline, not from someone else's discipline.

## Consider Physiological Factors

We need to point out one other angle on teens who seem to struggle with self-discipline. It's possible that a young person is experiencing real neurological limitations that produce what their parent sees as an unwillingness to stay on task. For example, many kids diagnosed with ADHD in their preteen years find that their symptoms worsen during puberty. That's especially true for tasks that require what's called "executive functioning," things like getting started, getting organized, and staying directed toward a goal. If a teen drops the ball in those areas, it's easy—but misinformed—to label them as lazy or undisciplined.

For some teens, the symptoms of ADHD and similar conditions may have been missed through elementary school and don't become fully apparent until a child is confronted by the challenges of high school. But whether a teen deals with ADHD or another challenge, we know that if they are freed to follow their inner motivation, true *self*-discipline will result.

# 17

................

# the emotional side of your child's giftedness

Along with all the other changes that are happening for your child during adolescence come a lot of new feelings, as well as new awareness of old feelings that have been lingering inside for a while. Not surprisingly, giftedness often factors into those emotions.

This topic gets very complicated, so we can't lay down any hard-and-fast rules. But it might help to point out three realities that come into play when we talk about feelings.

**Feelings by their nature are irrational.** That is, they do not stem from logic and reason, nor can they be understood or handled through logic and reason alone. That may seem obvious, but in some families (meaning, for some parents) rational thought and behavior are valued so highly that emotions are looked down on as a weakness. Indeed, in some families, feelings are simply not tolerated.

**People differ widely in how they experience and express emotions.** Some people are highly emotional by nature, while others have a rather narrow bandwidth of emotionality. Some people experience their feelings in a profoundly deep and all-consuming way, while for others, feelings come and go quickly. Some people let their feelings be known in no uncertain terms, while others remain inscrutable.

**The way parents process emotions will largely determine how they respond to their child's emotions.** Again, that dynamic may seem obvious, but perhaps for that reason it often gets overlooked. Remember what we said about your child doing something differently than you would do it? The instinctive response can be, "What's wrong with you?!" Nowhere is that question asked, if not spoken out loud, more than in highly emotional moments.

For instance, imagine a father who is by nature emotionally reserved, even stoic, and has never, ever shed a tear in front of his family. His son, Palmer, by contrast, is far more expressive and given to high highs and low lows. It doesn't take much to guess how those two will interact as the boy grows up.

Then one day when he is just shy of turning sixteen, Palmer gets a phone call from his drama teacher, informing him that the lead part in the spring musical, for which Palmer had painstakingly prepared and auditioned and had his heart set on performing, has been awarded to his chief rival.

Palmer hangs up and immediately erupts with despair and begins shouting, "No! No! It can't be! This isn't fair! That part was mine!" By now he's choking back sobs. "That part belonged to me. That was my one shot. Now it's gone. It'll never come around again. I'll just get left behind. My life is over."

To his father, this highly dramatic reaction seems completely uncalled for and over the top. In fact, it's downright unacceptable (to the dad). So he steps in—just the way he has stepped in countless times before—and says, in a tone that signals nothing if not disapproval, "Stop it! Stop it, Palmer! Stop with the crying. Pull yourself together and act like a man. What's wrong with you? This isn't the end of the world. You'll have other opportunities. If you don't quit, anyway. Quitters never win. Palmer, you just gotta accept your disappointments and move on. Acting this way isn't going to help anything."

To this father, the logic of this lecture makes perfect sense. But it's safe to say that if Palmer ever does reach his dream of becoming a professional actor and ends up winning an Academy Award, he won't begin his acceptance speech by saying, "I first and foremost want to thank my dad for this award, because he was there for me all the way. Thanks, Dad!"

> **A great deal of the damage parents do to their children stems directly from not being in touch with their feelings.**

Taken together, these three observations suggest that you as a parent should take inventory of your own relationship with feelings—first with your own, then with the feelings of others. A great deal of the damage parents do to their children stems directly from not being in touch with their own feelings, not being aware of emotional wounds they are still carrying from their past (including from their parents), and not respecting the emotions of their children.

## Giftedness Frustrated

Inasmuch as motivation is a form of desire, it follows that a young person will experience significant frustration when they are denied the satisfaction of fulfilling the thing they are born to do and most motivated to do. It's as if their whole reason for being has just been canceled.

You can see that in Palmer, just mentioned above, who has lost the lead in the musical. What is he born to do? Apparently his burning desire is to inhabit a role in a story and perform that part so convincingly that those who watch are compelled to enter that imaginary world. Doing that is when he feels most alive. That's when life makes the most sense to him. What's more, that's the best means he has of contributing to others. Quite literally, that is his *gift*—to them. Indeed, people thank Palmer for doing that. Audiences praise him for doing it. They celebrate his gift. His deepest desire translates into their delight. Everyone wins!

Palmer lives for the role and the story and the audience and the magic of the theater. Yes, there are so many other parts of life that he must attend to: eating, sleeping, doing math, babysitting his little sister, making his bed, helping his dad do yardwork, hanging out with friends, not forgetting to send a thank-you note to Grandma for the birthday present she sent him . . . All those things matter and must be attended to. But they all take a back seat to the energy that drives Palmer at his core: his motivational desire to act.

So when the call from his drama teacher says, in effect, "No, you can't act this time," he is devastated, emotionally. And, in keeping with his giftedness—which of course relies on his ability to experience, lean into, and portray a wide range of emotions as he plays different characters in different productions—he expresses his disappointment in a highly dramatic, oversized manner. What else would one expect from him, given who he is?

Someone with a different form of giftedness—and a different emotional makeup—would handle the frustration of their giftedness much differently. For example, take Wendy, a girl who comes alive at organizing the logistics, scheduling, and administrative details of an event. Wendy spends weeks meticulously planning out her club's service project. Then a freak thunderstorm the day of the project nixes the whole thing. Instead of crying and throwing a fit, Wendy goes right to work on a Plan B, making calls, handing out orders, doing everything she possibly can to regain a semblance of control and salvage what she can from nature's fickle ways.

Meanwhile, a placid, unflappable tenth-grade chemistry student named Jonathan delights in spending nights and weekends absorbed in journal articles posted online by PhDs in chemistry, physics, and related sciences. Jonathan is so quiet and reserved in his manner that his parents have nicknamed him The Ghost because he can come and go almost without being noticed.

At school, Jonathan's chemistry teacher wants to set him up with a special project to study what is known as Beer's Law, which states that the concentration of a chemical is directly proportional to the absorbency of a solution. However, to conduct the experiments for the research, Jonathan will need to obtain a device known as a colorimeter.

He doesn't have the money for that, so his teacher suggests he apply for a modest research grant from a foundation that supports STEM students in their high school studies. Jonathan spends the next week gathering lots of information to fill out a rather involved form, which his teacher then sends to the foundation.

A month later, Jonathan's teacher asks him to stay behind following chemistry class. In accordance with the foundation's policy, they have sent their response to the grant request to the chemistry teacher, and he has received their reply. "Jonathan, we've heard back from the foundation. I'm sorry to tell you, but they've turned down your request."

Jonathan takes in the news, expressionless, blinks, and then says, "Oh. Okay." Then he turns and leaves. He never mentions anything about this incident again. Instead, he goes right back to reading journal articles.

Was Jonathan disappointed? Actually, yes. Did he feel frustrated? You bet. But if anyone pressed him to find out his true feelings, he would simply say, "Yeah, it's a letdown. I thought it would be a cool project. But I figure I'll do it at some point anyway. For now, I think I'll ask my teacher if I can do this other project I've been reading about for determining the dissociation constant of an acid."

Three different young people. Three different forms of giftedness. Three different emotional reactions to being blocked in the expression of their giftedness. The point is that the frustration is real, regardless of how "hot" or "cold" the reaction may seem.

Having said that, we also know that if a young person's giftedness is repeatedly frustrated over time, their emotional health will suffer. Not just from repeated disappointment, which is bad enough, but even more by depriving them of the motivational "oxygen" they require from the regular satisfaction of their core desire. Quite simply: if you keep saying no to a child's giftedness, you'll squeeze the life right out of them.

## The Burden of The Gift

Every form of giftedness is inherently good, but every form extracts a certain emotional toll on the person who bears it. In other words, just by virtue of your child being who they are, they will experience certain emotional challenges related to their gift.

Earlier we met Jenna, the ultra-competitive girl who makes a contest out of everything. That's a great gift that could give her significant advantages if she ends up in a career like selling financial services or negotiating the terms of business deals. But that high-octane energy can also place a lot of stress on her system. It could predispose her to anxiety and/or fear of failure, especially if she finds herself handicapped by, say, an illness or a financial limitation. Another possibility is that she chronically worries as to whether she's "good enough."

We've also seen the dramatic reaction of Palmer to losing the part in the musical. So it's easy to see that he might struggle with depression and/or amplified feelings of self-doubt or diminished self-worth at times. Depending on how severe those moods become, he might start looking for ways to escape painful feelings through any number of self-destructive behaviors. That, of course, would only lead to further emotional struggles.

And then there's thirteen-year-old Claire, who has to be the kindest, most compassionate, sensitive, and generous girl that her middle school has ever seen. Claire is extraordinarily responsive to need. While her parents have never even heard of the term "giftedness," they absolutely know what hers is: "Claire Bear Care Bear" is the nickname they've given her.

It fits her well as she reaches out to the kids at school who get left behind, who have no one to sit with at lunch, who struggle with their schoolwork, or whose families don't have a lot of money. She comes alongside the classmate who looks discouraged. She lends a hand when a teacher has too much to carry. She immediately jumps in whenever volunteers are needed. In essence, she moves through her day instinctively looking around and asking the question, "Who needs my help? How can I make myself useful?"

So how could such a lovely gift cause emotional challenges for someone as cheerful, sweet, and optimistic as Claire? Well, what happens if Claire *isn't* needed? Or what happens if she just thinks she isn't needed? Might she interpret that to mean she isn't wanted? Or that she has no value? Or that she's done something to displease others? Give those kinds of self-doubts and fears some time to fester, and she might go further down a dark path of feeling that there are certain things she *must* do in order to be needed—many of which might not be in her best interest.

Claire might also conclude that her only value is in "being there" for others. In that case she might spend all her time people pleasing, to the neglect of what she herself needs or wants.

## Being There for Your Adolescent

Again, every gift has worth and is wonderful. But as your adolescent develops greater capacities for expressing their gift, they (along with you) will also discover some emotional side effects that are part of the package. That means they have to start learning to "manage" their gift, which in turn means learning to handle their feelings.

By "handling feelings" we don't mean denying feelings or just trying to stuff them away. That would be the worst thing to do! At their core, feelings are neither right nor wrong; they simply are. They tell us something about what's going on inside. So the first thing to do in handling an emotion is to be aware of it and acknowledge it and, if possible, put a name to it.

That's where you can be immensely helpful as a parent. Many adolescents haven't yet learned how to identify, own, and verbalize their feelings, let alone express them well. It's almost like they're back at age four or five, trying to learn to ride a bike. Emotionally speaking, they're pretty wobbly and unsteady, they fall down a lot, and they're going to get some bumps and bruises in the process. What they most need is someone to be there for them to steady them while they get their balance—and most especially to encourage them and reassure them that they *can* "do" this thing called feelings.

Notice, though, that as your child grows toward emotional maturity, *you also* will be on a growth curve. Just as your child has a lot to learn about their emotional life, you'll have a lot to learn about helping them with their emotional life. That will especially be so if you yourself have some emotional growing up left to do (as is the case for most young parents, and even a lot of older parents).

**Beware of assuming your child will go through adolescence the same way you did.**

The point is, as your child takes adolescent steps in their attempts to make sense of their feelings, what they most need is a safe place of unconditional love, which really means a safe person—hopefully you.

Which brings us back to something we said at the beginning of Part IV: your own experience of adolescence will likely affect how you parent your adolescent child. That can be good if it makes you a more compassionate, empathetic, and emotionally available parent. But beware of assuming that your child will go through adolescence the same way you did because by now you know that your child is different than you. Instead of guiding them solely on the basis of what you remember from that age, guide them according to Their Way. Look at this season of change and development through their eyes and help them find joy in growing up to be who *they* are born to be.

# PART V

# getting ready for liftoff

# 18

# looking for patterns of giftedness

Earlier in the book we met a little girl who liked to make up rhymes in her head while sitting at the playground. Later we discovered that her name is Danice, and her mother's name is Jaimie. We learned that Danice was described by one of her teachers as being "shy" at school. We also saw that Jaimie pursues parenting with relentless resolve, as if tackling a big challenge. So when Jaimie heard about the method of keeping a journal of her daughter's behavior in order to capture clues to her giftedness, she purchased a beautiful, hardbound journal to use in recording her observations.

On the first page Jaimie wrote, "Danice's Giftedness Journal." Then day by day she began to record brief entries about Danice and what she had seen her doing each day. Jaimie wasn't exactly sure where this project would lead, but she hoped it might somehow unlock what to her seemed like a mystery—who her daughter is.

## Danice's Giftedness Journal

Here are just a handful of the many entries Jaimie wrote over the years:

### *Danice as a Baby*

- I remember she had colic real bad. REAL bad. I thought I would go crazy! She gave me so many migraines. It took me weeks to figure out she was getting over-stimulated (I think?). "Infantile colic" is what they call it. All I know is, once we got rid of Thanos and things quieted down and I kept her room dark, she started sleeping more.

- Once the colic left she went to the other extreme. She would lie in her crib for hours just staring. No movements, no crying, just staring.

- Today I discovered a little game I can play with Danice. I say a word and then she says it. Then I say another word and she says that word. We go back and forth. Dog-dog. Cat-cat. Ball-ball. Cup-cup. Run-run. Hi-hi. She LOVES that game!

- Danice has taken to singing little song-like noises. Not with words that mean anything, but more like sounds that go together. Wee-wee, hee-hee, bee-bee, kee-kee. Olo-lolo-golo-holo. Woo-woo, koo-koo, noo-noo, boo-boo.

### *Danice in Preschool*

- I've started taking Danice to the playground down the street. I don't know why, because she doesn't want to play on any of the swings or the slide or the merry-go-round. But she likes going. She just sits and watches the other kids go back and forth on the swings and round and round on the merry-go-round. Strange.

- At dinner tonight Danice suddenly said, "Rain, rain, fall down, rain, rain, make sound." Then she just giggled. When she saw Jamal and me smile, she said it all over again. We couldn't stop her. She kept saying it over and over. She looked very pleased with herself.

- At the playground today I noticed that as Danice watches the other children, she seems to slightly move her head, almost like she's singing to herself.

- Tonight we got another rhyme at dinner. High, high, up to sky, down, down, toes on ground, run, run, fun, fun, fun.

### Danice in Elementary School

- Danice came home and told me she has to memorize a poem and recite it in front of her class. It's called "Chocolate for Breakfast." It's a pretty long poem. 5 stanzas. But she's already memorized the first three of them! She doesn't even have to have it ready until next week.

- Went to parents night at the school. Miss Crowder told me that Danice did a remarkable job reciting her poem in front of the class. She said she was really surprised because Danice is so quiet most of the time. But when she was in front of the class, she was like a different person.

- Today Danice brought home her report card. On it, Mrs. Knowlton wrote, "I have observed that Danice is a shy child, and for that reason I have not asked her to be in front of the class very much or to take any leadership roles." I have already left a message to see Mrs. Knowlton. There's no way Danice is going to be shy. Not my child!

- Today Danice told me she doesn't want to go back to school. I asked her why. She said Mrs. Knowlton divided the class into two teams for a spelling bee and made Danice the captain of one of the teams. Danice said she wasn't sure what she was supposed to do, and then when her team wasn't ready, some of the kids started laughing, and she started crying. So Mrs. Knowlton made someone else the leader. I told Danice she needs to start learning how to take charge and be a leader. Am I wrong?

### Danice in Junior High School

- We gave Danice a guitar for her birthday, which is what she said she wanted. She was so excited.

- Today I found a poem Danice had written for one of her classes. It was about bullying. I had no idea! A couple lines hit me really hard: "Don't you know when you call me that name, it cuts my heart with a knife of shame? Can't you see when you leave me out, I lose my way and I'm filled with doubt?" I asked Danice about this when she got home from school. She said she wrote it for an assignment. I asked her if she'd been bullied. She said a little, back in kindergarten and first grade. She said she used her experience to write the poem about some bullying that she's seeing at school now.

- I've managed to get Towlton Academy to admit Danice on a provisional acceptance. They're pushing STEM students, and that's not Danice's strong suit. But I pointed out that not every student is going to end up in STEM. I also showed them some of Danice's poetry and other writings. They were impressed enough to at least give her a chance. So here we go! Danice, girl, please don't let Momma down.

- Danice has fallen in love with her guitar. She can't wait to finish dinner and go to her room and play it.

- Today was the end-of-the-year awards assembly. Danice won the English award. I was so proud of her! Her English teacher, Mrs. Hester, told me that Danice wrote a story about a Chihuahua named Thanos, who became a famous rap artist and used his celebrity status to bring changes to the immigration system. Mrs. Hester said it was the most creative and thoughtful piece of writing she had ever received from a junior high student. "That girl has a future," she said. Later, I asked Danice about her award, but she was like it was no big deal. "They have to give an award to somebody," she said.

### Danice in High School

- The seniors at Danice's school are organizing a talent show. Danice says she entered her name to perform one of her songs. I told her not to get disappointed if they don't put her on the program, since she's only a freshman.

- A terrible thing has happened at Danice's school. I guess two older boys were hazing a freshman by forcing him to take an ice cold shower in the locker room. A coach walked in and when he tried to break it up, he slipped on the wet floor and hit his head. They took him to a hospital, but he died last night. The whole school is in shock. Danice hasn't said much of anything about it. She just went to her room to play her guitar.

- More bad news! Jamal has moved out on us. I have no idea what he's up to now. He says it's too expensive to have Danice in a private school, but I don't think this is about Danice at all. Something tells me he's been running around on me. Even if it is about the school, my baby deserves the best education she can get. When I told Danice her daddy was going to start

living somewhere else, she just said, "I'm sorry, Momma."
Then she went to her room and started playing her guitar.

- Tonight was the talent show, and Danice was the star of the show.
  My baby was the star! She sang a song she had written about
  the death of the coach in the hazing thing. She had that whole
  audience in her hand. People were crying. People were standing up, waving their arms. People were hugging each other.
  When she finished, she got a standing ovation and had to come
  back out and take a second bow. She MOVED that place!

- At breakfast, I asked Danice about the talent show last night.
  She said she thought it went well. I said, "Baby, it didn't just
  go well. You were the star! You brought that place down!" She
  said, "Really? I just thought people were being nice." Then
  she said, "I just want people to get it, you know, Mom?" I said
  get what. She said, "You know, how those boys being mean to
  that freshman boy ended up causing Coach Maynard's death.
  I mean, people can be so stupid at times. They don't get it that
  taking advantage of someone weaker makes all of us more
  vulnerable. That's why I wrote the song."

## Seeing Patterns

Hopefully, like Jaimie, you've been collecting observations of your
child's behavior over the past many years.[1] If so, the journal you've
compiled is worth gold! It contains lots of evidence that, when an-
alyzed and pulled together, can reveal invaluable insights into your
child's giftedness.

Remember, giftedness is a *pattern* of behavior—more specifically,
a pattern of *motivated behavior*. It's the behavior your child naturally,
instinctively, and consistently exhibits when they are free to choose an
activity and how they do it.

The way to identify that pattern is to look through the journal for words, themes, situations, and other elements that repeat and recur. Some of those elements will be obvious, and some more subtle. Some will be both obvious *and* subtle in the sense that it's easy to become so familiar with something in your child's routine behavior that you stop noticing it and start assuming it as a given. Specifically, you can look for the following:

**Abilities**. What abilities or strengths does your child display again and again when they are doing activities they enjoy? Some of these will be visible, such as writing, painting, reading, asking questions, speaking in public, playing a sport, or holding a conversation with someone. Others will be more internal or hidden: analyzing, brainstorming, setting a goal, making a decision, devising a strategy.

If we look through the entries above from Danice's Giftedness Journal, we find that Danice consistently uses abilities for rhyming, singing, telling stories, playing the guitar, composing songs, performing, and reflecting on difficult things that have happened. (There are likely others, if we had access to all of Jaimie's journal entries.)

**Subject matter**. What does your child keep working on, with, or through? We might call these elements "interest areas" because they are the things your child seems to be most interested in. In the last chapter we found Hank working with model rockets. Another child might show an interest in animals. For someone else it's numbers. For yet another it's a sport like basketball or soccer or cross-country.

Another way to identify subject matter is to look at a given activity and ask: What does my child use in doing this activity? They might be crafting a bowl using clay. They might be solving a problem using mathematics and numbers. They might be competing against someone using a game of chess and a strategy. They might be building something using tools, hardware, and materials. They might also be working with a person—for example, teaching little brother the alphabet or braiding a friend's hair. Or with a group—lining everyone up in a batting order or leading a group of singers.

If we look for Danice's subject matter, we find sound, and especially music, words and expressions, stories, emotions and feelings, the guitar, and also techniques for playing the guitar.

**Circumstances.** The circumstances are the conditions or environment in which an activity is taking place. Your child's motivation is like a plant. You can put a plant in different environments, and it will survive, but if you really want it to thrive, you place it in the ideal conditions for that plant. Likewise, when your child is doing an activity that brings them great satisfaction and energy, pay attention to the conditions in which that activity is taking place.

For example: Is it a team activity? Does your child seem to do better when there is some kind of structure and rules? Do they seem to come alive when confronted by unexpected demands, crises, or emergencies? Do they like working toward a goal? Do things have to be hard enough to engage their motivation—so that they come alive when the circumstances are challenging and putting their skills and wits to the test? Is there danger or risk? Does it appear that some sort of response or feedback from others seems important? Is there some sort of objective scale by which your child's performance will be evaluated—a score, a grade, a ranking? Are a lot of your child's best moments happening mostly outdoors? Is there a model or mentor or guide involved?

Circumstances are more difficult to notice than abilities or subject matter because they are outside your child, not inside. They can easily become so assumed that they go unnoticed. It's like a fish not really paying attention to the fact that it needs water to thrive. So you have to look carefully at the journal entries and ask, what does my child seem to need in order to thrive?

If we ask that question of Danice, we find that she operates best in conditions like solitude, time to reflect, time to practice and prepare, and where there is an audience of listeners or readers. We also notice that Danice's gift especially comes alive in response to a problem or crisis, a situation where something meaningful needs to be said.

**Role**. When your child is doing an activity they enjoy, what role do they tend to play relative to the other people in the activity? Suppose your child thrives in group and team activities. Are they the leader or captain who takes charge? The rah-rah, talk-it-up, get-everybody-excited cheerleader of the team? The "clutch" player who wants to be indispensable? The reliable but often inconspicuous "team player," who quietly but faithfully just does their job? The brains of the group who always seems to have the great suggestion?

Of course, you may find that your child is an individualist who prefers to do things on their own, even if it's in the context of a group.

From Danice's Giftedness Journal entries above, we can see that Danice is such a person.

**Satisfaction.** If you've gotten into the habit of asking your child to describe what they find satisfying about a given activity, you should have lots of evidence from their Giftedness Journal to identify the driving satisfaction of their motivational makeup. Whatever it is, that satisfaction is the motivational outcome that their abilities, subject matter, circumstances, and role are working together to allow them to experience.

We've talked about the countless possibilities for what might drive a child's behavior. But here are a few examples of what various parents have found for their child:

- Janelle loves to set a challenging goal that causes growth, either in herself or others.

- Keenan is determined to win by finding ways to use his strengths at the point of someone else's weakness.

- Chad thrives when he is immersed in what he defines as a "solution," which usually means figuring out how to make something work better.

- Xavier is born to get all the facts, listen to all the opinions, think through all the options, and weigh out all the factors in order to present a persuasive explanation of what is actually going on.

- Tisha just wants to be part of a team. She doesn't really care what the team is doing (as long as it's not something bad). She just wants to play her part in helping her team succeed.

- Ashley's delight is to lead a team in accomplishing a challenging project where the skills of many different people are needed and the outcome can make a profound difference for others.

- Thomas seems most alive when he's outdoors, working on a team, in challenging conditions, and the clock is ticking.

As Jaimie looks through Danice's Giftedness Journal, she sums up Danice's consistent satisfaction like this: Above all else, Danice wants to know she has "connected." She loves to experience the world, reflect on what it all means, and then present her insights through some creative expression that allows others to "get" it (her words).

# 19

# your child's pattern as a whole

Putting your child's Giftedness Pattern together is a lot like working on a jigsaw puzzle. A jigsaw puzzle is composed of a lot of individual pieces, but it's the big picture of the completed puzzle that lends context, and therefore meaning, to any individual piece. You can't just lift one piece out of a jigsaw puzzle and say, "Here's the puzzle." No, that's a piece of the puzzle, but only one piece among many.

The same holds true for your child. You can't point out one, single dimension of their giftedness and try to describe the whole of who they are through that one piece. Yet we hear parents do that all the time: "Sam is a numbers guy." "Maria is a bookworm." "Wallace is a talker." "Sofia is a people person."

Descriptors like that are one-dimensional. Your child is a whole person, and their giftedness is an organic whole. Sam may well be a "numbers guy," but where do numbers fit into the rest of who he is? What does he do with numbers? For what purpose? Under what circumstances? And what does he find so satisfying about working with numbers?

In order to keep that bigger, integrated picture of your child's giftedness in view, we recommend that you pull together the elements of your child's pattern into a succinct, one-page summary. Here is Jaimie's summary of Danice's pattern to illustrate what that looks like:

## DANICE'S GIFTEDNESS PATTERN

**Danice uses her abilities for. . .**

rhyming
singing
telling stories
playing the guitar
composing songs
performing
reflecting on difficult things that have happened

**to work on, with, or through. . .**

sound
music
words and expressions

stories

emotions and feelings
the guitar
techniques for playing
the guitar

**in circumstances that provide her with. . .**

solitude
time to reflect
time to practice and prepare
an audience (listeners, readers)

a situation where something
meaningful needs to be said

**and in the role of. . .**

an individualist

**in order to gain the satisfaction of. . .**

experiencing the world, reflecting on what it all means, and
then presenting her insights through a creative expression
that allows her to "connect" with others, so that they "get"
it (her words).

There you have it! An overall description of Danice when she is living in the "sweet spot" of what she is born to do. Her Giftedness Pattern is like her own personal "owner's manual." Yes, there are many other things that Danice can do, does do, and must do. But this is what she most desires to do and what she does best. It's what she was born to do. That's what Danice's mother needs to pay the most attention to as she parents Danice.

It's also what Danice needs to pay attention to as she looks toward graduating from high school and making choices about her life and career. Hopefully she can end up in work that fits her giftedness. But she might not. Either way, her giftedness will never fundamentally change, so it remains the trump card in how she decides to navigate her way through life.

You can write out your child's Giftedness Pattern on a piece of paper or create a computer document. Or use the form that we've created.[1]

## Celebrating the Pattern

Hopefully you've been pointing out and affirming different bits and pieces of your child's giftedness from the time they were little. For example:

- When your child was a baby, maybe you responded to her delighted giggles by saying, "Oh, baby likes that! Fun, fun! Yes, baby Lucy loves that!"

- When your boy was a toddler, proudly "paving roads" and "moving mountains" in the backyard with his little Tonka toy bulldozer, you shouted out, "Connor, what a highway! Look how straight you graded that road!"

- Maybe when your seventh grader volunteered to take care of the class bunny over the winter break, you told her, "Kelsey, how

## _____ **GIFTEDNESS PATTERN**

_____ uses his/her abilities for. . .

to work on, with, or through. . .

in circumstances that provide him/her with. . .

and in the role of. . .

in order to gain the satisfaction of. . .

wonderful of you to take responsibility for the rabbit! You really care for creatures like no one I've ever seen."

- Or when your fifteen-year-old wrote a paper on the theory that Caliban, a beast-like character in Shakespeare's *The Tempest*, is a portrayal of how seventeenth-century Europeans viewed people from other continents and cultures, you remarked, "Isaiah, you seem to have a real knack for taking complex subjects and making them clear and understandable."

Now that your child is older and you have a robust description of their Giftedness Pattern, you have a wonderful opportunity to show them your findings. We like to call this "celebrating the pattern" because that's what it should be—a celebration of who your teenager is and what they do best. "Celebration" conveys the idea that your teen's pattern is something positive, that it's important, it matters, and those who love the teen should share in the joy.

Having said that, you can read your child to decide on the best way to celebrate their pattern and show them the underlying data from their Giftedness Journal. With some teens, it's enough to just say, "Hey, son, I've got something to show you. You know that journal I've been keeping all these years about observations of your giftedness? Well, I sat down with it the other day and looked it over. I'd love you to see what I discovered."

With another child, you may want to make it a much bigger moment, perhaps tying it in with a milestone event, such as your child's sixteenth birthday. After discussing their pattern with them and talking about some of its implications, you might mark the occasion with a special meal.

You might also consider celebrating their giftedness through some tangible gift that symbolizes or aids them in the pursuit of their unique bent. For instance, to a girl like Danice, for whom singing is such a key part of her pattern, Jaimie might buy her a couple of tick-ets to a concert by one of her favorite vocalists. Or for a boy in New Jersey who has immersed himself in the world of investing, his father might take him to visit the New York Stock Exchange. Or for Hank, the young man who builds rockets, his folks might buy him a photo of a SpaceX Falcon Heavy spacecraft signed by Elon Musk. Or for the girl mentioned above who has brought home the bunny, her folks might give her a new lionfish to add to her aquarium.

Later we'll say more about helping your teen learn to use their Giftedness Pattern and apply its implications. For now, we just want to stress that the pattern you've developed for them is not just your opin-ion of their strengths and motivation. It is based on objective evidence from their own lived history. In fact, if you've been careful to record some of their own words in real time—meaning when they were in the moment of using their giftedness—then they ought to instantly recognize themself in what you show them.

## Your Child Is the Expert on Themself

But of course, that leads to a very important point: the only person who really knows whether the pattern you've generated seems accurate is your child. By this age, they definitely should be able to tell whether the person you're describing is the person they know themselves to be. That means you have to hold the pattern with a degree of humility because they may push back on parts of it. Remember, the giftedness is in *them*; the pattern is merely your best attempt to accurately describe what is in them. But that description may fall short. That's okay. It's a work in progress.

Some adolescents are particularly sensitive about parental intru-sion. And no one wants to be put in a box. So if your teen disagrees with any of your conclusions, let them have their way—although, as we said above, your conclusions should be based on objective evidence that you can show them if they'd like. People are frequently surprised when someone shows them examples of their actual behavior. They've never noticed that behavior because they live inside their skin.

But living inside their skin works the other way, too. There are things they experience and perceive that you don't see. For example, only they know what feels satisfying and energizing to them. You tend to see them through the lens of what matters to you and how your giftedness operates. So it's always possible that you've ended up assigning a different meaning to what you've observed than for what is actually true for your child.

We see that all the time in our work. A parent will remind their young adult child about the award they received at the high school honors assembly. "That was your big moment!" the parent will say. But in fact, the child never cared about the award. They were infinitely more proud of the short story they wrote their senior year that helped them win that award.

Parents have an especially challenging assignment if their child is a person of few words or if they're highly selective about what they share with their folks. Their teen may have been keeping a lot of motivational clues under the radar, as it were—not so much trying to hide anything, but more that it just never occurred to them to bring anything up.

## A Work in Progress

So hold your conclusions lightly. And whatever you do, don't try to force your child to accept the pattern you've developed on them. Anyone who does that should be sued for parental malpractice! Like we said, the pattern is a work in progress. Not the giftedness, but your *description* of the giftedness. You've developed a first draft, not a finished product. Your teen is still young. They haven't yet had much of an opportunity to express their giftedness in adult ways. So with time and more experience, more "evidence" will show up, enabling you (and them) to refine their pattern.

Think of this process as if you're watching a garden over a long time. Certain plants in the garden bloom earlier or later than others, and some flourish only in particular seasons. Some are perennials that just keep showing up year after year, others come and go. Some trees lose their leaves in the fall; others remain evergreen. Over time, the enduring plants tend to grow bigger and stronger, and they dominate the garden.

Note that all of the original land in the garden remains in place. But with time, you have so much more growth to observe, so many colorful plantings and mature vegetation. It all comes to life and enhances the beauty of the garden. In a similar way, all the various aspects of your child's giftedness will show up over time, enhancing the wonder and the beauty of the person you see.

# 20

# are they ready?
# are you?

B y now your child is somewhere around sixteen, seventeen, maybe eighteen years old, and the time for them to leave home will soon be at hand. "Leaving home" is analogous to a rocket ship lifting off from the launch pad and (hopefully) rising up through the atmosphere to begin its journey to the stars. In the end, you'll have spent eighteen years, give or take, preparing your child for that momentous send-off. But just as Mission Control runs a myriad of evaluations and spot checks before initiating the T-minus sequencing for countdown, so you as a parent will (or should) find yourself asking: *Is my child ready to go?* After all, no parent wants to see a "failure to launch."

## What Your Child Has Going for Them

*Is* your child ready to go? If you're like far too many parents today, you may answer that question by skeptically shaking your head and muttering something like, "Are you kidding? No way! We've done the best we could, but I think my son/daughter is going to get a rude awakening when they get out in the real world." Too often that comment is said in a tone that almost expects the child to—maybe even *ought* to—fall flat

235

on their face as they take their first steps into the adult world.

For your child's part, you may be surprised to know that they may actually be wondering themself whether they're ready to commence their journey into the future. Sure, they may display a brave and bold demeanor that signals they think they've got things pretty much figured out. But deep down inside where no one can see, they likely harbor a bit of self-doubt, and perhaps even anxiety: "Do I *really* have what it takes?" (Remember how you felt at their age?)

If you've been intentional about raising your child according to The Way of Your Child—which means you've worked the process of discovering, celebrating, and honoring their giftedness, and then helped them discover and own and lean into their giftedness—then we believe the answer to your question ("Are they ready?") as well as theirs ("Do I have what it takes") is undoubtedly *yes!* Because if you've paid attention to raising your child as a person instead of a product, they now possess at least ten key assets going into the future:

(1) Confidence in their core strengths. They know a lot about what they are capable of doing, given the right circumstances.

(2) An awareness of the subject areas and activities that most interest them and motivate them. What a great thing to know in a world filled with endless options!

(3) The beginnings of an idea about a direction they'd like to pursue. Maybe not quite a vision for their life yet, but at least some notions about a path to start checking out.

(4) Insight into how they learn. That's invaluable for any future education they'll encounter—whether formal or informal, whether academic or otherwise.

(5) A grasp of which activities and scenarios "work" for them—which ones have their name on them, so to speak. They can make wise choices, moving toward options that fit them and

where they'll likely excel, and steering clear (as much as possible) from options that don't.

(6) An understanding that in all likelihood they need to be on the lookout for models and mentors to help them grow and develop. They can be intentional about finding those people, not just luck into them—or not.

(7) An "owner's manual" (their Giftedness Pattern) with which to navigate the many opportunities and challenges that lie ahead. That objective appraisal of their gifts is a valuable means of bringing them back to the "good truth" about who they are.

(8) The comfort and security of knowing they have a parent(s) who believes in them and is *for* them—even if that parent is very different from them. They can rest in the knowledge that their parent is willing to let them "be who they be."

(9) Their giftedness itself. It is *always* there and always *will be* there, ready to do what it's made to do. It's the best of who they are. Their sweet spot.

(10) A purpose for why they're here.

## Living on Purpose

Let us dwell on that last point for a moment, because that's where the real pay dirt lies. We've told you from the outset and all through the book, so it makes sense that we would leave you with this thought: your child has been placed here for a purpose. They are here to make a contribution to the world.

Life is not about finding a job or even a career. Yes, yes, life involves earning a living and taking responsibility to provide for oneself and one's family. And since work takes up the bulk of one's waking hours, why not seek work that *fits*—that is, that makes good use of one's gifts. And yes, more and more people in this world are discovering options for doing very purposeful work, which we think is wonderful!

But as our father reminded his students so often, a career is what you're paid to do, whereas a calling is what you're made to do. That's why we encourage you to encourage your child to seek a vision that goes beyond a paycheck into the very reason for why they wake up every day. The wellspring of that reason will always flow out of their giftedness, and for that reason has the potential to be quite fulfilling. But personal satisfaction is not *why* they have the gift. No, its purpose is *to cause the world and its people to flourish in some signature way.* As Helen Keller put it so well, true happiness in life "is not attained through self-gratification but through fidelity to a worthy purpose,"[1] by which she meant a purpose beyond oneself.

Your child is still young, and they will be the rest of their life learning about the nature of that purpose. But now is the time for them to get started on that learning adventure—if nothing else, to simply be aware that their life is a gift, and they bear a responsibility to *give* that gift to others, to exercise it on behalf of others. By that means, they will end up loving people with the *best* of what they have to offer.

## Are You Ready?

But now, let's turn things around and talk about you, the parent. As the days on the calendar slip by and the moment of send-off grows closer, are *you* ready? We don't mean, are you ready for them to leave? Rather, *are you ready to continue parenting them well once they leave?* That's the real question, because parenting doesn't end when your child is gone from the home; it just transitions to a different season in the relationship.

The dynamics of parenting your adult child are far too involved to get into in this book. But our experience with countless parents whose cherished eaglet has finally flown the nest suggests that at least one dominant emotion you may be feeling at this point is fear. Yes, you're excited for your child's new independence, and you (hopefully) have high hopes for them as they pursue the next stage of their journey. But you know in your gut that they have to live out their life in this crazy thing called The Real World. And that world is looking crazier and scarier by the day!

At the start of the year in which we wrote this book, we never imagined that our message would be born in a time when all the peoples of the earth would be forced to let go of the familiar certainty of things as they had been and instead be exiled into the foreboding shadowlands of a global pandemic. That scourge has taken the lives of millions and stolen the dreams of hundreds of millions. Which vastly complicates the already complex task of parenting: How do you encourage your young adult to seize the day and make the most of their life when you don't even know what the world will look like after the pandemic and all of its contemporaneous crises—whenever "after" finally arrives?

As parents ourselves, there are days right now when we, perhaps like you, find ourselves lamenting, "I fear for my children, and for my children's children."

So how does one parent in a scary world? Well, just as certain kinds of stories reveal human giftedness, so certain stories reveal bedrock realities that can provide great comfort in troubling times.

One such tale is *The Last Battle*, the seventh book in *The Chronicles of Narnia* series by C. S. Lewis. That story comes down to a climactic showdown. On one side are the devoted and true followers of Aslan, the great lion-king who rules all of Narnia. Aslan, we are told, is by no means safe—but he's good! He's the King! Indeed, he's the image of what a king should look like. On the other side are the malevolent forces of an evil pretender posing as the king, who threatens to annihilate all of Narnia. His troops severely outnumber Aslan's cohort, led by brave Tirian, the last monarch of the kingdom. Battle is joined, and Tirian quickly finds himself hopelessly outmaneuvered. In short order, all appears to be lost.

## You and Your Child Are Held

As they stare into the void of an all-but-certain defeat, one of Tirian's intrepid band of soldiers fearfully inquires what will happen to them. To which Tirian somberly replies: "There's no knowing." A defeated silence falls over the group. And then Tirian pronounces these most profound and moving words: "But courage, child: we are all between the paws of the true Aslan."[2]

Held between the paws. That safe space of belief and expectancy in the midst of doubt and uncertainty, sensing that we are overseen by the benevolent presence of a loving being. It is the experience of *being home* that each of us longs for as a child and never stops looking for our whole life. It is a hope that tethers us to something larger, to a haven that will save us, even in the worst that life—or even death—throws at us.

Where can we find the paws that are holding us in times like these? The popular tendency is to try and predict (an attempt to control) the future, to bring order to our next steps by looking ahead. But an ancient tradition suggests just the opposite—that the best perspective is often gained by looking backwards. A Hebrew poet wrote: "Remember His wonders which He has done, His marvels and the judgments spoken by His mouth."[3] Whenever the people needed help collecting their bearings in lands without landmarks, they would picture themselves as in a rowboat, their backs turned away from the scary and uncertain future as they rowed, while they kept their eyes firmly fixed on *where they had been and what had been provided for them there*. In that posture, they gained great courage by "remembering the wonders," telling each another the stories of how they had received great blessing and unexpected provision in moments when all seemed lost.

If you've practiced our process of collecting the Giftedness Stories of your child—as well, if you've gone through the exercise we recommended for telling your own Giftedness Stories—then you have an abundance of evidence that you and your child both have been held between the paws throughout your lives. Those Golden Moments when you got to live out and express that wonder-full thing called your giftedness is a sure and reassuring token that you are here for a reason. And though life may shake you to the core, it can never nullify your purpose for being.

We can think of no better place to make camp and set your heart at rest in what certainly feels like hostile territory right now. When you brought your little one into this world, you embarked on a bold and self-sacrificing journey. And whether you realized it or not, you your-self have served as the paws for your child in this world. Our premise is that—aware or not—you and your child have been led on through the many hours, days, and years of not-knowing by a purpose woven throughout all that you both have been uniquely made to be.

The light of your child is just now beginning to be seen, to be expressed, to illuminate the presence of a brand new mystery. As that happens, there will be days for you—no parent alive can truthfully declare otherwise—when the fear and worry of not knowing how it will all come out will almost overwhelm you. At times, it will seem that you can never find the way to get this parenting thing right, and your only certainty is of how many mistakes you've made and keep making along the way. But know this: even when the night presses in to keep the light from getting through, your child's story *will* be told.

Scientists tell us that when we look up at the night sky and see the Big Dipper, we are seeing light from stars that originated eons before we were even born—stars that contributed the very elements we find in our solar system, in our planet, and in every human being. All of that points to the notion that we are, each of us, participating in an unfathomable mystery in which we play some inextricable part that is meant to be. In that story, the cycles of life determine that daylight will inevitably fade, and the dark places will find us. Yet the light remains, hidden in plain sight—emanating from the wonder of each life that is born. One of those lives was chosen for you to unwrap as the precious gift it is. So cherish your privilege: to you was given the unique joy of being the first to discover, in the fullness of time, the worth and wonder of the person called Your Child.

# acknowledgments

Books usually have only one or two named authors, but they all have countless contributors. That's because while one or two individuals write out the words that come from within, their message and their understanding of it flows out of a mighty river of relationships that the authors have been swimming in over a lifetime. As authors, we have been indelibly marked and generously enriched by countless people, but we want to name some of the more prominent influences on what we have penned in this book.

The first and most enduring thanks go to our parents, Howard and Jeanne Hendricks. We would point out that even though we are siblings raised in the same family, there's a sense in which we did not have the same parents. Different birth order and gender, along with the unique ways in which either parent responded to our giftedness, and we to theirs, made for significant differences in our experiences. But one vital lesson we both learned from them about parenting is that it is not about trying to get everything "right," but to keep showing up—even when, at times, it means sacrificing one's own desires. We have not been the easiest children to raise, but in the end, they allowed us to "be who we be."

Both of us have families of our own, and so we want to express our thank-yous to our children—Bev's daughters, Alison, Megan, and

Lauren; and Bill's daughters, Brittany, Kristin, and Amy. We feel like they've taught us more than we ever taught them. Those privileged connections only continue to reveal to us, in real time, what parenting is *really* all about!

And for Bev, with the added blessing of a new generation, comes the joy of being Nana to six delicious grandchildren. She has the high privilege of being present to the wonder of giftedness that can only be theirs—all the while watching her girls be the amazing mothers they are and learning so much from their example. It has become one of the humbling graces of her life.

Bill must also add his deep and abiding appreciation for the way in which Nancy, exemplary mother to their three daughters, parented them according to The Way of the Child. She instinctively knew pretty much everything we've written in this book long before Bill ever did, and the difference she made in the days she was given is a legacy we will carry in our hearts and lives forever.

Both of us have also been blessed with countless mentors and guides. One whose input and personal investment in us transformed this book was the late Gladys Guy Brown, who happened to be the first licensed female psychologist in Dallas County. From the very moment she heard about the phenomenon of giftedness, she became a champion for our work and one of the wisest counselors we were honored to have known.

So where did we learn about giftedness? We should especially name three of the pioneers in this area: Bernard Haldane, Art Miller Jr., and Ralph Mattson. We've also benefited from dozens of mentors and colleagues at People Management, Inc. and its successor, SIMA® International, Inc. (now SIMA® II, LLC).

But our greatest learnings have come from our many clients over nearly three decades at The Giftedness Center. This book is not only our truth, but theirs, as well. It's an account from the holy ground of their personhood, revealed to us through the mystical power of their Giftedness Stories. We are indebted to and enriched by every single one of them for generously trusting us with those most cherished recollections. We simply could not have written this book without their gracious participation.

Specifically in terms of giftedness in parenting, we are especially grateful for the model of our very treasured friends, (the late) Tracy Wood, his extraordinary wife, Carol, and their five sons, all exemplars of giftedness: Asher, Nelson, Fulton, Leighton, and Taylor. How many times have we come away from watching Tracy and/or Carol interact with their boys and remarked to each other, "Now *that's* how you pay attention to giftedness as a parent!"

Bill wishes to say a huge thank you to his mother-in-law, Carol Turpin, for the gracious hospitality she showed in allowing him to spend the better part of the summer of 2020 at her summer home in the Smoky Mountains of North Carolina. It proved to be the perfect setting for writing his part of the book. (It also gave him an escape from Texas's summer heat, as well as a refuge from the growing pandemic.)

Bill also expresses deep appreciation to his longsuffering wife, Lynn, whose giftedness for doing things together was sorely tested and frequently frustrated by Bill's solitary habits when he went into writing mode. Her patience, understanding, and encouragement are as much a contribution to the finished product as anything Bill brought to the book.

It is impossible for Bev to imagine a better companion supporting her, advocating for her, and always believing in who she is than her husband, Dale Godby. He provided unknown resources, thought partnership, and a listening ear all along this journey—beginning as her mutual partner in parenting; becoming the devoted and beloved father to their own three girls, and later as Papa to their adoring grandchildren; and finally, undergirding this writing odyssey with the kind of emotional and tactical support that has made it all possible.

The team at Moody Publishers have been friends of our family for a long, long time. So it's been a pleasure to partner with them once again on yet another publishing project. Duane Sherman "got" this concept right from the start and acted as a superb sponsor all the way from getting it greenlighted through the final production process. Betsey Newenhuyse used the skills of a surgeon in trimming away a lot of excess material in order to turn the manuscript that we submitted into a much leaner, stronger book.

To our agent, Bob Hostetler, at The Steve Laube agency, thank you for all of your help and guidance to get this project placed with Moody.

Finally, we want to acknowledge that giftedness is called what it is because it's a gift from the One in whom St. Paul said "we live and move and have our being."[1] We are each profoundly grateful for the gifts we've been given, and whatever benefit anyone receives from this book, the thanks belongs, not to us, but to the Gift-Giver.

# notes

**An Invitation**

1. "Tremendous Trifles," in *Tremendous Trifles* (London: Methuen & Co., 1909).

**Chapter 1: Meant to Be**

1. "Ode on Intimations of Immortality" from *Recollections of Early Childhood.*

**Chapter 2: You're Parenting a Person, Not a Product**

1. "NBAS," Boston Children's Hospital, http://www.childrenshospital. org/research/centers-departmental-programs/brazelton-institute/ nbas. See also T. Berry Brazelton and J. K. Nugent, *Neonatal Behavioral Assessment Scale* (Cambridge, MA: Mac Keith Press, 2011).

2. Ibid.

**Chapter 3: The Indelible Signature of Giftedness**

1. For those who were born after about 1970: a slide rule was what engineers and others working with equations used before electronic calculators and computers were invented. A slide rule resembles a common foot-long ruler, but it is not used to measure things, but rather to do mathematical calculations and functions.

2. Bill Hendricks, *The Person Called You: Why You're Here, Why You Matter & What You Should Do With Your Life* (Chicago: Moody Publishers, 2014), 28.

### Chapter 4: Five Things Parents Need to Know

1. Lin-Manuel Miranda composed the 2015 Broadway smash hit, *Hamilton: An American Musical*, based on the life of Alexander Hamilton. The third song from Act 1 is entitled, "My Shot," in which the words, "I am not throwin' away my shot," are used almost entirely throughout the song. The idea is that Hamilton intends to make a future for himself and not squander his life.

### It Starts with You

1. The System for Identifying Motivated Abilities (SIMA®) is a proprietary and very disciplined protocol for examining people's history of meaningful achievement in order to describe patterns of motivated behavior, or giftedness. SIMA® is owned by SIMA® II, LLC, Omaha, Nebraska. Bill Hendricks and The Giftedness Center is a licensee of SIMA® II, LLC.

2. "Discovering Your Giftedness: A Step-by-Step Guide," The Giftedness Center, http://www.thegiftednesscenter.com/discovering-your-giftednesstitlegyd.

### Chapter 5: Nurturing the Heart of Your Child

1. "Shy," Merriam-Webster's Collegiate Dictionary, 11th ed. (Springfield, MA: Merriam-Webster, 2003), https://www.merriam-webster.com/dictionary/shy. https://www.merriam-webster.com/dictionary/shy.

2. Proverbs 22:6 NET.

### Chapter 6: First Look

1. Just to be crystal clear: when we use the term "energy" we are not describing something mysterious or magical or metaphysical like the Force in *Star Wars*. Motivational energy is the personal, internal impulse that moves or drives someone to do something.

2. For more on intrinsic and extrinsic motivation, see Edward Deci and Richard M. Ryan, *Intrinsic Motivation and Self-Determination in Human Behavior*: Perspectives In Social Psychology (New York: Plenum Press, 1985).

3. If you would like to keep a Giftedness Journal for your child online, visit http://www.giftedness.co/parenting. In addition to that online journal, you'll find additional resources related to giftedness and parenting.

4. For more information on Tom Landis and Howdy Homemade, see https://howdyhomemade.com/locations.

## Chapter 7: The Golden Years

1. "The Weekend Song," Fred Rogers,1970.

2. Fred Rogers, *You Are Special: Words of Wisdom for All Ages from a Beloved Neighbor* (London: Penguin Books, 1995).

3. *Audubon: The Making of an American* (New York: Alfred A. Knopf, 2004), 4–5, 143. Alice Ford, Audubon by Himself (Garden City, NY: The Natural History Press, 1969), 4. Alice Schroeder, *The Snowball: Warren Buffett and the Business of Life* (New York: Bantam Books, 2008), 94, 117–18. "Tammie Jo Shults," Wikipedia, last edited May 23, 2021, https://en.wikipedia.org/wiki/Tammie_Jo_Shults.

4. Etch A Sketch was invented in the late 1950s by a French electrician named André Cassagnes. He named the device *L'Écran Magique* (The Magic Screen). Eventually The Ohio Art Company bought the rights and renamed the toy the Etch A Sketch. It quickly became the most popular drawing toy in the industry. Today, it is owned by Spin Master Corporation of Canada, and there is an electronic version of the toy featuring colors and sound effects through a controller attached to a video screen.

## Chapter 10: Setting Expectations

1. History.com Editors, "Albert Einstein: Fact or Fiction?," October 27, 2009, updated June 4, 2020, https://www.history.com/topics/inventions/einsteins-life-facts-and-fiction.

## The Barbie Doll Dream House

1. Frederick Buechner, *The Alphabet of Grace* (New York: HarperOne, 1989), 60.

2. James 1:17 NIV.

### Chapter 13: The Essence of Adolescence

1. Carl E. Pickhardt, "Fearful Parenting of Adolescents," *Psychology Today*, February 28, 2011, https://www.psychologytoday.com/us/blog/surviving-your-childs-adolescence/201102/fearful-parenting-adolescents.

### Chapter 15: The Priceless Presence of Models and Mentors

1. Charles C. Seifert, *The Negro's or Ethiopian's Contribution to Art* (Black Classic Press, 1986).

### Chapter 18: Looking for Patterns of Giftedness

1. Remember, you can keep a Giftedness Journal for your child online at http://www.giftedness.co/parenting. You'll also find additional resources there related to giftedness and parenting.

### Chapter 19: Your Child's Pattern as a Whole

1. You can find a copy of the Giftedness Patterns form online at http://www.giftedness.co/parenting.

### Chapter 20: Are They Ready? Are You?

1. *Helen Keller's Journal, 1936–1937*, Journal Date: December 10, 1936 (Garden City, NY: Doubleday, Doran & Company Inc., 1938), 57–58.
2. C. S. Lewis, *The Last Battle*, in *The Chronicles of Narnia with The Lion of Judah in Never-Never Land*, by Kathryn Lindskoog, vol. 2, (New York: Religious Book Club, 1973), 101.
3. Psalm 105:5 NASB.

### Acknowledgments

1. Acts 17:28 NIV.

# about the
# authors

**Bill Hendricks** is cofounder and president of Global Centre for Gift-edness, which seeks to mobilize a worldwide movement of Giftedness Guides—people who know how to help others discover their gifted-ness and then apply those insights to the major areas of their lives. This is an outgrowth of his longtime consulting practice, the Gifted-ness Center, which helps individuals think through strategic life and career decisions. In addition, Bill serves as the Executive Director for Christian Leadership at The Hendricks Center, a leadership devel-opment initiative of Dallas Theological Seminary. He holds degrees from Harvard University, Boston University, and Dallas Theological Seminary, and is currently a doctoral student at Bakke Graduate Uni-versity. He is married to Lynn Turpin Hendricks and is the father of three grown daughters.

**Bev Hendricks Godby** is a senior associate and change management coach at The Giftedness Center in Dallas, TX. She particularly focuses on graduating students and women of all ages who are navigating the uncertainties of challenging transitions by helping them to reclaim and actualize the "good truth" of who they are to move their lives forward with purpose and meaning. At the heart of all she does, Bev feels called to her role as educator, kindling the love of learning about giftedness to help others find their best and most fulfilling lives. In addition to her assessment and coaching with individual clients, she serves as a consultant to several schools and nonprofit organizations, and enjoys conference speaking and writing on this topic. She holds degrees from Wheaton College and the University of Texas at Dallas. Bev is married to Dr. Dale Godby, with whom she has three married daughters and six grandchildren.

# TheGiftednessCenter™

*www.thegiftednesscenter.com*
*www.giftedness.co/parenting*

## BILLHenDricKS.neT

# Here's more help for parenting your unique child!

Parenting was never intended to be a solo activity. Yet in the daily routines of raising a child, it can be easy to feel alone, confused, and left wondering, "Do I *really* know what I'm doing here?"

We totally understand! Both of us are parents, and we well remember how it felt to encounter one new situation after another where we didn't know what to do. That's why we've created a special set of online resources just for you as a parent. You can find them at. . .

**www.giftedness.co/parenting**

We want to expand the usefulness of this book by taking the conversation deeper. Think of us as your own, personal Giftedness Guides when it comes to parenting—devoted advocates committed to walking alongside you as you raise your child.

At www.giftedness.co/parenting, you'll find. . .

- **Your Child's Giftedness Journal,** where you can keep a password-protected, online record of your child's motivated behaviors (as described in Chapter 6). This section includes more instructions and examples on how to keep the journal, helpful questions to ask, and other guidelines for capturing the invaluable clues that point to your child's giftedness.

- **Mondays with Mom,** a blog devoted to matters of mothering.

- **Podcasts** featuring interviews with seasoned parents who understand the value of giftedness and how it affects the raising of children.

- **Bev and Bill's Inbox,** a way for you to contact us directly with questions, comments, stories of what's happening with your child, and other inquiries.

- **Frequently Asked Questions,** a growing database of our answers to common questions about parenting and giftedness.

- **Additional resources** that we're adding on an ongoing basis to help you and your child thrive!

Our aim is to spark a global movement of parents who are raising children according to giftedness—The Way of Their Child. Check it out today and join us at. . .

**www.giftedness.co/parenting**

# IF IT WEREN'T FOR HIM,
# I WOULDN'T BE THE MAN I AM TODAY.

**MOODY
Publishers®**

*From the Word to Life®*

*Men of Influence* teaches you the importance of mentoring, how to find a good mentor, and what you can offer others as a mentor (even if you don't feel qualified). People change one person at a time. Realize your full potential and help others do the same through the simple practice of mentoring.

978-0-8024-1359-8  |  also available as an eBook